The Radar Book

The Radar Book

Samuel M. Van Wyck and Max H. Carpenter

WITH ILLUSTRATIONS BY JOAN B. MACHINCHICK

Cornell Maritime Press : Centreville, Maryland

Library of Congress Cataloging in Publication Data

Van Wyck, Samuel M., 1931-
  The radar book.

    1. Radar in navigation.   I. Carpenter, Max H.,
1921-   II. Title.
VK560.V36   1984   623.89′33   84-45261
ISBN 0-87033-326-7

Manufactured in the United States of America

First edition; second printing, 1994

With respect and affection,

this book is dedicated to our friend and teacher,

Captain Wayne M. Waldo,

United States Merchant Marine (Ret)

Contents

Preface

Welcome to *The Radar Book.* If you are the skipper or navigator of one of the large or very large vessels afloat on the world's waters today, this book is a must for you. Its nontheoretical approach makes the text accessible as well to the recreational mariner who utilizes a small radar on his craft.

Since radar was first developed, computer technology, the transistor and integrated circuit, stabilization, and, of course, ARPA (automated radar plotting aids) have all improved the usefulness of the equipment. So important has this new technology become for navigation and maritime safety that indeed, in some cases, vessels may not even enter certain harbors unless they are equipped with *two* radar sets.

On the other hand, despite all the advances that have been made in the plotting and observing capability of the radar equipment, it still remains the task of the captain, mate, or operator of the vessel to use and interpret the data properly and to be able to apply it so as to insure the safety of his vessel as well as the safety of other vessels in the vicinity. It is our hope that this book will provide new insights and all the basic information needed by radar users. Before getting on with the business of radar, a few acknowledgments are in order. Since both authors are presently employed at the Maritime Institute of Technology and Graduate Studies in Linthicum, Maryland, Max Carpenter as Chief of Simulation and Sam Van Wyck as Chief Radar Instructor, we naturally owe a large debt of gratitude to the two thousand or so students upon whom these theories and techniques have been practiced and refined. Much of what you read here has come as the result of suggestions or criticism from the students themselves.

What would a book of this type be without illustrative material? The beautifully executed diagrams are the work of Joan Machinchick of the Lake Claire Design Studio. Joan's patience and suggestions were essential to the completion of the book. She is an outstanding calligrapher and indeed, some of the scratched notes on the outside of file folders and bits of scrap paper were works of art by themselves!

Finally, credit is due those unsung heroines who made it possible for the authors to do what they had to do without worrying about where the next meal or clean shirt was coming from. To Harriet Van Wyck and Evelyn Carpenter, million de gracias!

The authors will welcome reader questions, as well as comments or suggestions for improvement. A letter or card to the publisher in Centreville, Maryland 21617, will reach us, and you can be assured of a reply.

S. M. VW.

M. H. C.

The Radar Book

1. Relative Motion

Unfortunately for the radar operator relative motion is an abstract, something that isn't at all obvious and therefore a bit hard to deal with. Consider two ships steaming on a calm sea, or imagine two ship models on a chart. One ship moves north at 20 knots. The other ship heads east at 20 knots (Figure 1). Their projected courses meet, but will they collide? To determine that, you need to take a series of ranges and bearings from one ship to the other. If the bearings remain constant while the ranges decrease, a collision is possible.

Figure 1 shows what is basically a true motion or pictorial presentation. As you can see, the track lines of the two vessels will cross ahead; a collision is possible. Will the two vessels arrive at the point of intersection at the same time? Will they collide or pass clear? The answers to these questions are to be found by determining the relative motion that exists between the two vessels.

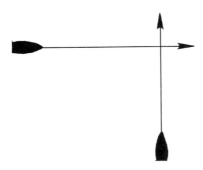

Figure 1. Plan view (true motion).

One means of establishing the relative motion and thus, the risk of collision, is to take a series of ranges and bearings from one vessel to the other over a period of time. How to obtain this information from your radar and use it properly are the major purposes of this book.

If you were to observe the situation in Figure 1 on the relative motion radar of the ship at the bottom of the picture, you would see a track similar to that in Figure 2. Since this is a relative motion radar, the track information that you see is also relative motion. Your ship's position is fixed at the center of the display, and the other vessel's bearing is more or less constant while the range decreases. This is indeed a collision or close quarters situation requiring little or no interpretation by the radar observer.

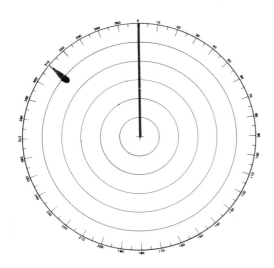

Figure 2. Collision situation as seen on a relative motion radar.

Relative motion is valuable because it is the part of the plot that tells you whether or not your ship is going to be involved in a collision. In fact, this situation may be stated, however inelegantly, as the theorem:

Relative motion is what runs over you.

And this leads us immediately to a second theorem:

Successful collision avoidance is the management of relative motion.

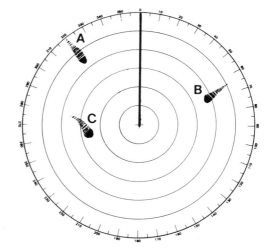

Figure 3. Ship A: Collision; Ship B: Passing clear astern; Ship C: maneuvering to avoid collision.

Figure 3 demonstrates this theorem. Target A's relative motion radar track indicates a collision situation is possible, while Target B's relative motion track shows that it will pass well clear. Target C, on the other hand, shows a change from a collision track to passing clear, indicating that it maneuvered so as to change its relative motion. Target C's maneuver illustrates the second theorem in which a change in the relative motion can be seen to reduce the risk of collision.

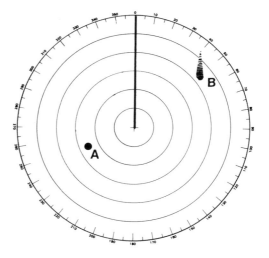

Figure 4. Relative motion can be confusing! Target A is steaming north at 20 knots while B is not moving at all!

What are the disadvantages of relative motion? Figure 4 shows one of the more annoying problems. Objects that are stationary, dead in the water, are seen to move. Buoys, land masses, ships at anchor; all show motion on the radarscope. On the other hand, a vessel on the same course and speed as yours, even

4

though you might both be whipping along at 35 knots, shows no motion at all! That vessel just sits there. This can be confusing until you become familiar with each situation. Furthermore, in order to know the course and speed of another vessel, you have to plot them because the radar track does not show this information. Nevertheless, whatever its disadvantages, relative motion is supreme when you need the answer to the question, "Is this vessel a threat to mine?"

2. The DRM Rules*

**All plotting methods that follow assume
either the use of an azimuth-stabilized
radar or the proper use of a transfer plot.**

MANEUVERS BY RADAR

One of the pleasures of teaching collision avoidance radar is being present when a student has a sudden breakthrough or "revelation" about something. Most often this brings on a slow smile, but occasionally, it impels the more emotional types to stand up and "testify" to their new awareness. Neither of these reactions is obligatory if you should experience anything like this during the course of reading this book!

The rules for maneuvering by radar, when understood, are the most common cause of a student's "revelation." These rules are nothing new. If you've had the responsibility of the bridge and have ever had to maneuver your ship to avoid another ship or to pass a buoy, you have used the maneuvering rules. However, in order to avoid confusion between the Rules of the Road and their associated rules for maneuvering, we'll refer to the following as the DRM (direction of relative motion) rules. The direction of relative motion is the way in which a target is seen to move on a stabilized relative motion radar. (For a complete discussion of radar operating modes, please turn to Chapter 8.)

Figure 5 shows the reaction of two targets to speed change maneuvers by your vessel. Target A, originally on collision course, will pass ahead clear of your vessel in response to slowing or stopping. Target B, also initially on collision course, will pass astern if you increase your ship's speed. This very predictable response of a target's relative motion track leads to the first two DRM rules.

**Rule 1. When you reduce speed, stop, or
stop and go astern, *all relative motion
tends to move upscope.***

**Rule 2. When you increase speed, *all rela-
tive motion tends to move downscope.***

This brings us to another definition, and a most important one. What, exactly, is meant by *upscope* or *downscope?*

In Figure 5, *upscope* would be toward the top of the page; the top of the radarscope. Any direction of relative motion from one degree above horizontal to vertical, or parallel to the headflash, would be considered *upscope. Downscope,* on the other hand, would refer to any direction of relative motion between straight down, parallel but opposite to the headflash, to one degree below horizontal in either direction. This is easily shown in Figure 6. Here, targets on the left side of the screen are *upscope* targets while those on the right side are all *downscope.*

What about stabilized radar in which the headflash moves to indicate a change in course? Easy, if you remember that wherever the headflash points, *there* is the *top* of the scope. Heading south? Then 180° is *up* and 000° is *down.* This can be mighty confusing until you get used to it. Just remember: up is wherever the end of the headflash is, and it's a prudent mate who, in the beginning, checks his observations by walking around the radar so that the headflash may be seen pointing away, in the natural "up" position.

---

*DRM rules, i.e., direction of relative motion rules, were first used by Max Carpenter and Wayne Waldo in *Real Time Method of Radar Plotting* (Cornell Maritime Press, 1975), 75.

6

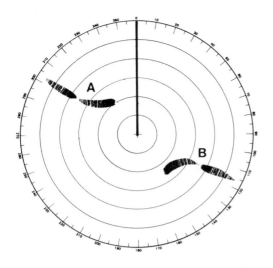

Figure 5. The effects of a speed change are easily observed on a relative motion radar.

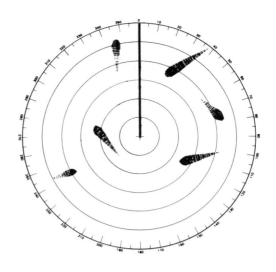

Figure 6. Targets to port are *up* targets; To starboard: *down.*

THE DRM RULES FOR COURSE CHANGE

Having mastered the rules for speed change, look at what happens when your ship changes course. Figure 7 shows a target (Quick, is it an up- or downscope target?) on collision course. A right turn to approximately 70° would produce the reaction shown in Figure 8. As your headflash moves from 000° right toward 70° (remember, you are assuming the use of stabilized relative motion radar), the DRM of the target changes *clockwise*, or to the right as viewed from behind. (In all these discussions, a change *clockwise* will be referred to as being "to the right.")

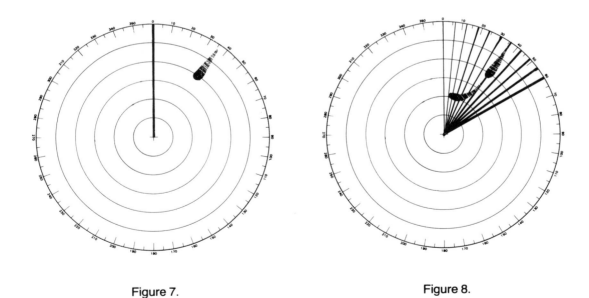

Figure 7.

Figure 8.

A *down* target . . . changes its DRM to the *right* (clockwise) when your ship turns to the *right.*

7

The same initial situation is seen in Figure 9 but with a planned avoidance turn to the left. The result of the left turn, seen in Figure 10, is a change of relative motion in a counterclockwise direction, or to the left. (DRM changes *counterclockwise* will be referred to as being "to the left.")

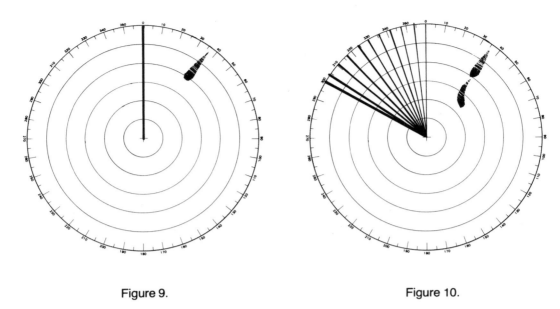

Figure 9.   Figure 10.

A *down* target . . . changes DRM to the *left* when your ship turns to the *left.*

From this discussion then, you may draw another conclusion to be incorporated into the DRM rule book:

**Rule 3. When your ship changes course, a
down target will change its direction of
relative motion *in the same direction that
your ship changes course.***

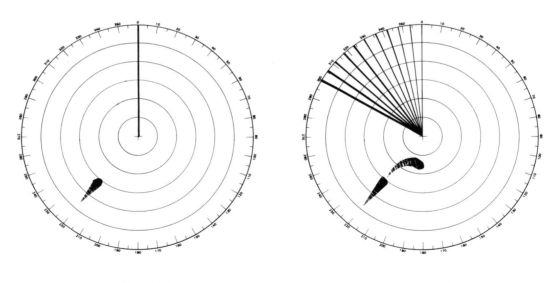

Figure 11.   Figure 12.

An *up* target . . . changes its DRM track clockwise to the *right* when your ship turns *left.*

8

Figure 11 again depicts a target on collision course. (Once more, is it an upscope or downscope target?) Right the first time—an upscope target it is! Now, if your ship turns *left* to avoid this threat, the DRM of the target will change *clockwise* or to the right as you see in Figure 12. The same target in Figures 13 and 14 will change DRM to the *left* or *counterclockwise* if you maneuver to the *right*. You can easily see that up targets are rather contrary types, and this leads to:

Rule 4. An *up* target will change its direction of relative motion *opposite to the way your ship turns*.

Remember, if you turn right, an up-target's DRM will change to the left, or counterclockwise. If you turn left, it will change to the right, or clockwise. You might say, sort of as a reminder, that *up* targets go *opposite*! Sorry about the bad pun, but it does help to remember.

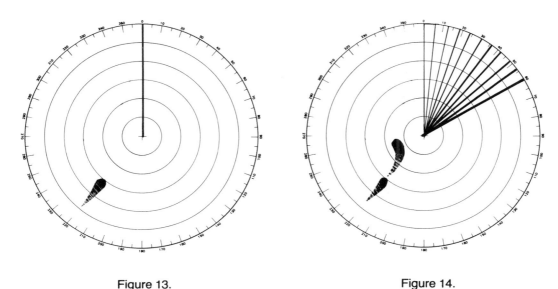

Figure 13.   Figure 14.

An *up* target . . . changes its DRM counterclockwise, *left,* when your ship turns *right.*

So far, only targets whose relative motion has been upscope or downscope have been considered. There is a third class of target whose DRM is neither. Figure 15 shows several targets whose DRM is

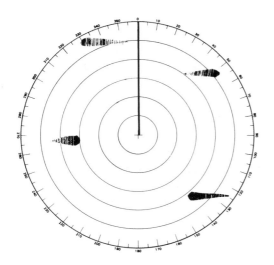

Figure 15. Limbo targets.

exactly at a right angle to your headflash and thus, is neither upscope nor downscope. This target was first described by Carpenter and Waldo as a *limbo* target.* There are several basic facts about the limbo target that you will want to know, but for now consider only the first two:

Rule 5. Depending upon the direction of your turn, the limbo target will become either an upscope or downscope target and will react accordingly (as in Rules 3 and 4).

Rule 6. Any maneuver you make (excepting a speed increase) against a limbo target *will cause the target to go upscope, relative to the initial position of the headflash.*

Figure 16 shows two limbo targets reacting to a 60° right turn by your ship. The initial position of your headflash was your heading prior to any maneuver or 000°. As the turn proceeds toward the final course of 60°, the DRM of the targets will be seen to change in accordance with Rule 5. Also, both targets change DRM upscope relative to the original heading in accordance with Rule 6.

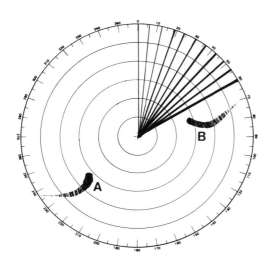

Figure 16. Rules 5 and 6.

After you steady up on your new heading of 60° you will note that the prediction of Rule 4 has come to pass. Target A is now an *up* target while Target B is distinctly *down,* as observed in the new top-of-the-scope position of 60°. Since these targets are no longer in limbo, they will follow DRM Rules 1 and 2 governing upscope and downscope target reactions.

You should note also that had you reduced speed, the reaction of Targets A and B in Figure 16 would have been very much the same as observed for the course change. What would have happened if you had increased speed? Both targets would have changed their DRM downscope.

To review what you have so far: Course and speed changes by your vessel result in predictable changes in the DRM of targets on your radar. Slowing or stopping causes all DRM to change upscope while a speed increase will cause all DRM to tend downscope. In response to your ship's course change, a *down* target will change DRM in the same direction as your turn. An *up* target will change DRM opposite to the direction of your turn.

*Real Time Method, p. 75.

Now, one more item before going on to plotting techniques. While all targets will react as described in response to your ship's maneuver, there is still the matter of how much reaction to expect. The higher the SRM (speed of relative motion), the less effect your maneuver will have toward changing the DRM. As you will learn, the SRM may be obtained from plotting, but it is also easily observed and estimated on the radarscope by noting the length of the target's "tail," the path of light left behind the target on the screen. Figure 17 shows two down targets responding to a 45° right turn by your ship. Target A has a high SRM and is only slightly affected while Target B, having a lower SRM, is very strongly affected. Simply stated, those fast ones are tough to push around!

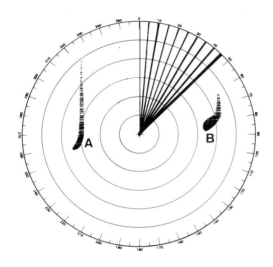

Figure 17. Effects of a course change against targets with different speeds of relative motion.

11

3. The R—T—M Plot

Manuvering by the use of the DRM rules is an essential skill for the deck officer. However, both the Rules of the Road and the demands of good seamanship require that skill be acquired and maintained in the art of radarscope plotting. A competent officer will make full use of eyeballing a maneuver with the DRM rules as well as direct plotting. Most important is the knowledge of which one to use in a given situation.

Rapid radar plotting is best performed when using a direct plot "reflector scope" mounted directly over the radar screen. If this is not available or if an unstabilized radar is being used, the plot is best done using a plotting sheet with corrected data from the main radar. Since the majority of vessels today have at least one stabilized, direct plotting radar, the emphasis here will be on the reflector scope method.

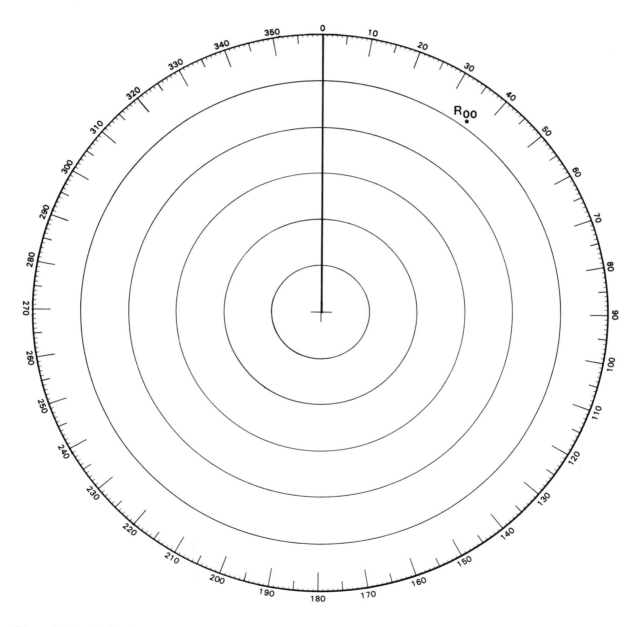

Figure 18. Beginning the R—T—M plot with R.

THE BASIC RADAR PLOT

The basic radar plot to be described here utilizes the R—T—M triangle, first described by Carpenter and Waldo.* It is constructed on the radarscope first by placing a reference mark over the target. This point is labeled R, and the time of the observation, in minutes, is placed beside it (Figure 18). In these next pages, we shall assume that all initial observations are taken at local midnight, time 00, unless otherwise noted.

As you observe the motion of the target's image, you begin to get an appreciation of its movement relative to your own ship's position at the center of the scope. After a given interval, three minutes in this case, you note that the target has moved to another position on the radar screen. Mark this with a second dot, labeling it M and marking the time 03 beside it (Figure 19). These two letters, R and M, mark the *relative motion* of the target. That's easy, isn't it? As a matter of fact, from these two observations alone, you can derive four important facts about the target vessel. These are:

1. DRM (direction of relative motion): A line drawn from R to M gives you the DRM of the target.

2. CPA (closest point of approach): Extending the relative motion line toward your own ship's position at the center of the scope gives you the value of CPA. If the line does not pass through your position, indicating that the target will pass clear, you may measure the CPA by drawing a second line from scope center to where it meets the relative motion line at a right angle (Figure 22). The length of this second line is the CPA value. In Figure 19, the CPA value is zero.

3. SRM (speed of relative motion): The speed at which the target image approaches your vessel's position at the center of the scope is called the speed of relative motion or SRM. This value may be measured directly, using the appropriate speed scale and plotting interval, or it may be easily calculated. In Figure 19, the target image has traveled one and a quarter miles during the three-minute observation period. Thus its SRM is 25 knots. (For reference, Time-Speed-Distance Scales are shown in the Appendix, Table 2.)

4. TCPA (time of CPA): The time at which the moment of CPA will occur is the TCPA. In the case of a collision course target, it's the time you'd hear the crunch!

As far as the basic R—T—M plot is concerned, there are only two other values to be obtained, but for these, some additional plotting is needed. You've observed the development of relative motion and marked the points R and M. You also know your ship's course and speed which will be north at 20 knots. In order to show this value in the plot, you use a line that will be labeled T—R. This line represents your ship's course by pointing north and has a length proportional to your speed of 20 knots (Figure 20). Your radar is on the 6-mile range, and so each ring is 1 mile wide. You've used a 3-minute plot for R—M, and so you must use the same interval for T—R. Three minutes at 20 knots is one mile.

Where do you put T—R in the plot? Already, you have the points R and M marked so put the R in T—R on the Point R already plotted. Since T to R indicates north, Point T should appear one mile south of R. The rule for the proper placement of T is that it always falls astern of R, parallel to the headflash.

In fact, the line R—T represents the track an object would follow if thrown overboard from the other vessl at time 00. Three minutes later, in the plot you're constructing here, it would appear one mile to the south of R at Point T.

*Real Time Method, p.1.

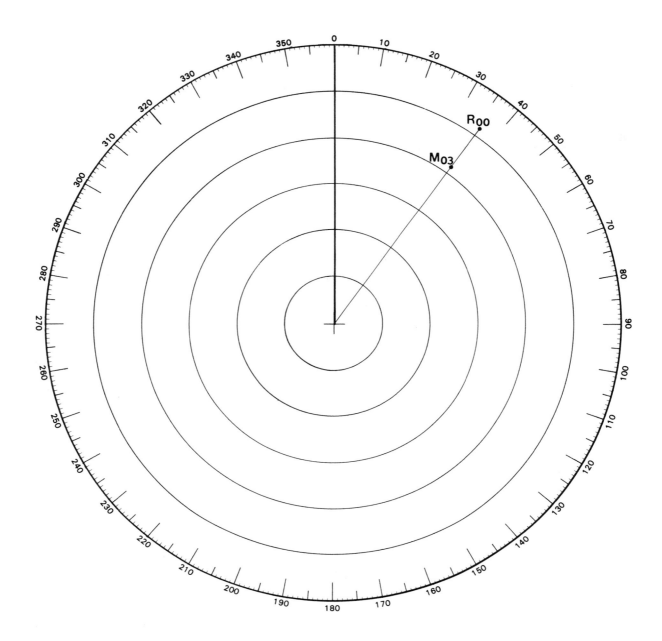

Figure 19. Step Two: Placing M.

14

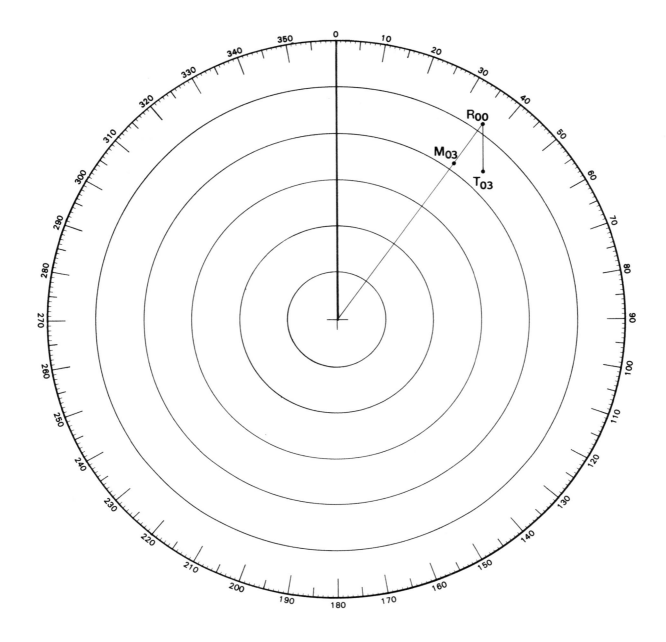

Figure 20. Step Three: Placing T astern of R, parallel to the headflash.

15

If you now combine the plots shown in Figures 19 and 20, you create the composite seen in Figure 21. The R—M side of the plot shows the approach of the target, the DRM, CPA, and so forth; the T—R side describes the course and speed of your ship and finally, the T—M side shows the *true* course and speed (*true motion* or *target motion*) of the other vessel. These values may be obtained by paralleling the T—M line with the parallel grid cursor (PGC), shown as a light line and arrow, in order to read the DTM and by measuring the distance traveled between T and M during the 3-minute plot period. The distance here is about ⅔ mile so that the speed of the other ship (STM) will be about 13 knots. The DTM is about 286°.

Basically, what you have just done has been to construct two known sides of a triangle and from these you can complete the unknown third side. The final two values obtained are:

5. DTM (direction of true motion): The course of the other vessel.
6. STM (speed of true motion): The speed of the other vessel.

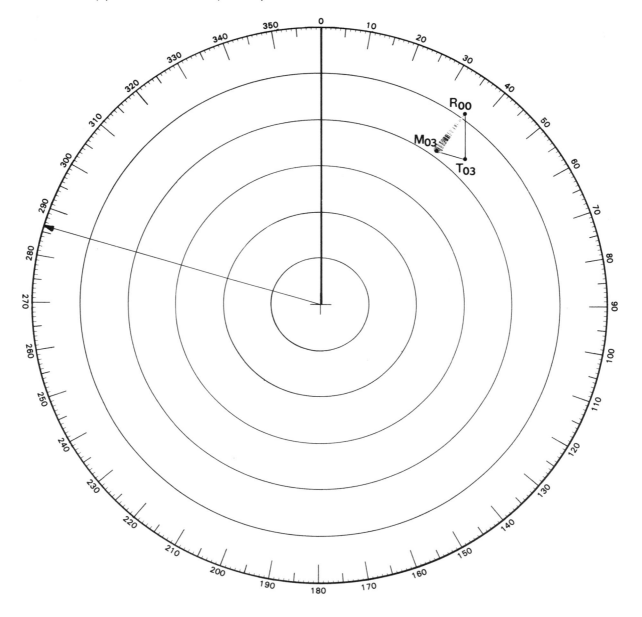

Figure 21. The R—T—M plot revealed! The other vessel's heading is about 286° as shown by the light line parallel to T—M.

RADAR SCALE AND PLOT INTERVAL

In the preceding example (as shown in Figure 21), the scale of the radar was set to six miles, and a plot interval of three minutes was used. This relationship of six miles and three minutes is no accident. Virtually all modern radar has a standard series of ranges and range ring spacing. These are designed to make the selection of plotting interval and the measurement of speed and distance simple and error free. The following table will show you the way it is set up.

Radar Scale and Plot Interval Table

Range (nautical miles)	1½	3	6	12	24	48
Plot interval (minutes)	¾	1½	3	6	12	24
Number of rings	6	6	6	6	6	6
Ring interval (nautical miles)	¼	½	1	2	4	8
Distance travelled by a 20-knot target in one plot period	¼	½	1	2	4	8
Number of rings a 20-knot target travels in one plot period	1	1	1	1	1	1

First, you see that the radar is arranged so that each scale doubles, or halves, the one next to it. Each scale has six rings; this never changes. No matter what scale you choose, a 20-knot vessel *always* travels exactly *one range ring* distance during the plot period. The plot period is *always* half of the number of the range scale in use. This way, you always know what plotting interval to use: 6 minutes on the 12-mile range, 24 minutes on the 48-mile range, 45 seconds on the 1½-mile range, and so forth. Since the distance traveled by a 20-knot target during a standard plotting interval is always one range ring, you can use a single speed/distance scale for all your measurements on the radar, regardless of the range you are using. This standard will be observed throughout the book.

Figure 22 is a standard 6-inch plot sheet suitable for practice work. Two plots have been initiated. Your ship's course is north at 20 knots. Using a parallel rule or triangles and divider, try solving for the 6 values, DRM through STM on each plot, and compare your answers with those given (see below). Do not split degrees or knots; whole numbers are more than adequate. Your answers should come within about 10 degrees, 3 knots, 3 minutes, and, for CPA, about ¼ mile of those shown. If they don't, make certain you're following the letters of the plot (R to M for relative motion; T to M for true motion) in their proper direction and that you are using the speed scale or time-speed-distance formula correctly.

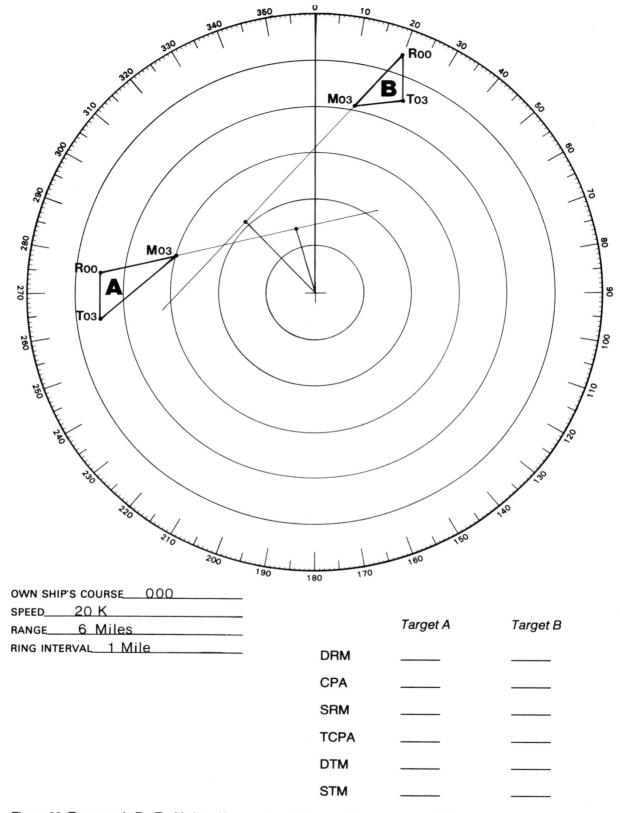

OWN SHIP'S COURSE ___000___

SPEED ___20 K___

RANGE ___6 Miles___

RING INTERVAL ___1 Mile___

	Target A	Target B
DRM	_____	_____
CPA	_____	_____
SRM	_____	_____
TCPA	_____	_____
DTM	_____	_____
STM	_____	_____

Figure 22. Two sample R—T—M plots. (Answers to plotting exercise are on page 82.)

18

4. Plotting a Maneuver

Having mastered the basic R—T—M plot, you will now begin to put this knowledge to use as you calculate course and speed changes for collision avoidance.

SPEED CHANGE

Basically, you need to ask yourself two important questions when plotting a maneuver: "What is happening *now*?"; and "What is it that you *want* to happen?" In Figure 23, you plot a target that is obviously on collision course, and so it's easy to see what's happening *now*. Since collisions at sea are likely to be detrimental to your health and career, you must decide what it is you want to have happen instead. You *want* the target to clear your vessel, and the first collision avoidance maneuver to be covered will be stopping your ship.

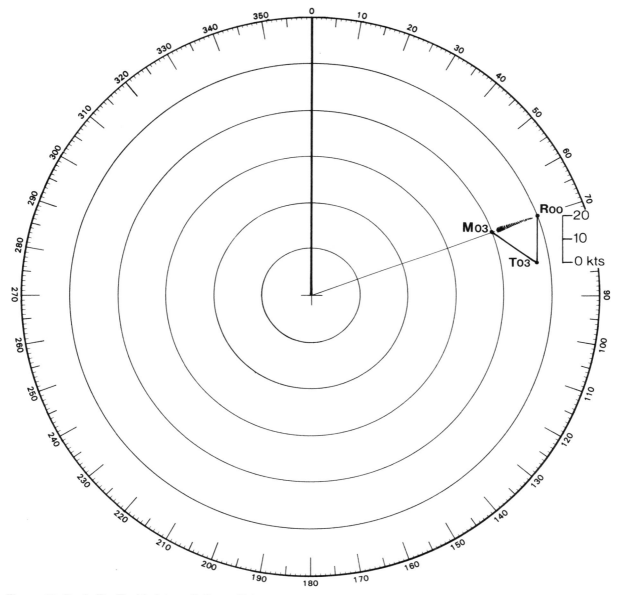

Figure 23. Basic R—T—M plot predicting collision.

Referring again to Figure 23, you see that your ship's course and speed are indicated by the direction and length of the line T—R. Now, here's a very important point to remember when calculating a speed change maneuver:

The point "T" is always considered to be zero speed reference.

The speed of your ship, or the target vessel, is always measured using T as zero knots and measuring away from T. For instance, you can see right away that our ship is presently making 20 knots. The quantity "20" is measured, starting at T, from T to R. Point R is 20 knots distant from T.

Now, in order to indicate slowing or stopping your ship, Point R must be moved toward T. Reducing the distance between R and T is the equivalent of reducing the plotted speed of your ship. To *stop* your ship, move R all the way down to T so that there is zero distance between them. This gives you the plot in Figure 24.

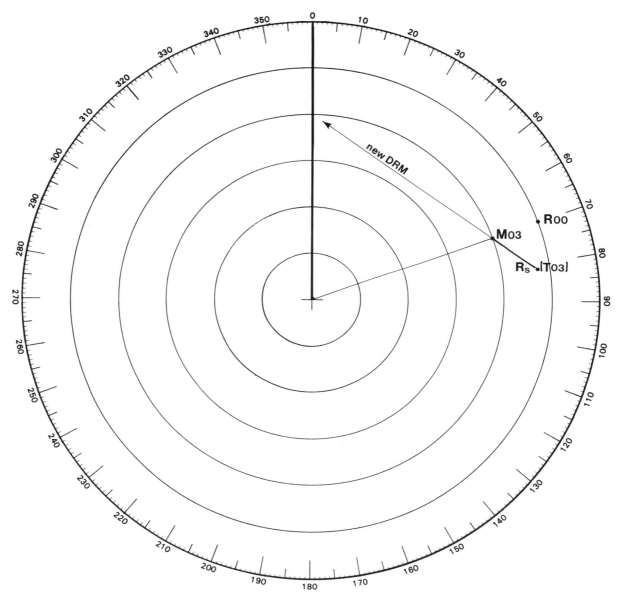

Figure 24. R—T—M plot showing the result of stopping your ship.

With Point R resting on top of T, your ship is stopped. Now, what happened to that DRM line that was predicting collision? Reading from point Rs (the "s" indicates a (s)peed change) at its new location, through M, you now see that the DRM line, thus the track of the other vessel, clears your ship by over three miles. Stated briefly, this plot tells you that if, at time 03, you were to reduce the speed of your ship from 20 knots to zero knots, the DRM of the other vessel would change from an indicated collision to a CPA of over three miles.

Here's another point about the "stop" plot. Note that when you stopped your ship, the new DRM line became the same as the true motion line. Since Points R and T are together, the lines R—M and T—M are also together and thus, the relative motion and true motion of the target on your radar have become the same. This gives you a very handy rule to work with:

When you stop your ship, all relative motion becomes the same as the true motion.

While making rules, add one more:

Never move T!

Remember that when you reduced the speed of your vessel in the first example, Point R was moved toward T. Never do it the other way around: moving T toward R. Why not? Because in the plot, T is shared by your ship, showing your course and speed, and by the other ship as well, as part of the indication of its course and speed. Were you to move T, you would be changing the course and speed of *both ships!*

Suppose, instead of stopping, you merely slowed to 10 knots, what would your plot look like? To find out, move R toward T until it is opposite the 10-knot mark. The new DRM and CPA are then easily seen by connecting R and M as shown in Figure 25. Want to increase speed? Simple! Increase to 30 knots by placing R opposite the 30-knot index. Again, read the new DRM and CPA between R at 30 knots and M. Slowing your ship moved the DRM line to pass the target ahead while increasing speed dropped the DRM line to pass the target astern.

One more point to consider before finishing the discussion on speed changes for a while. Up to now, only the results of a specific, predetermined speed change have been considered. Suppose, however, your question is "What speed must I come to in order to make the target pass a *specific* distance away? Can I make it pass exactly one mile ahead or astern?" Sure you can. All it takes is a slight change of method. Look at the plot in Figure 26.

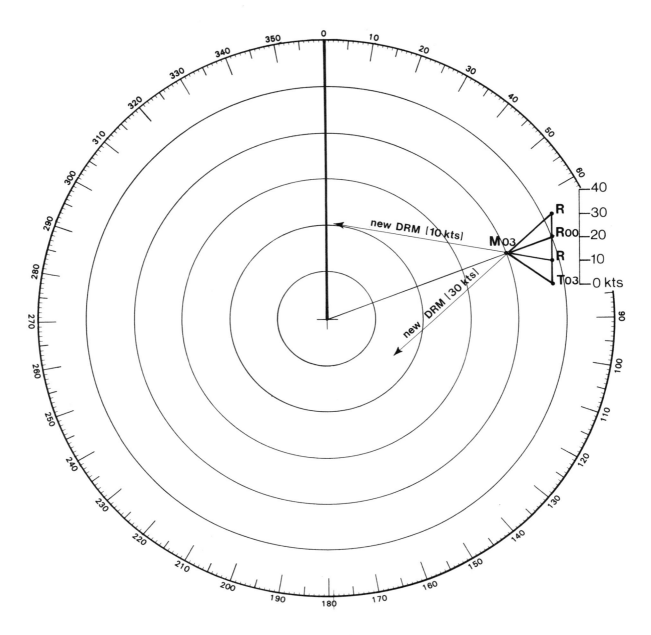

Figure 25. R—T—M plot showing the result of various speed changes.

This time, the new DRM lines are drawn from Point M 03 (the location of the target at minute 3 in the plot) to the one-mile range ring ahead and astern of your ship. These are the new DRM lines you would like the target to follow after you slow or increase speed. What changes are needed to make all this happen? Note that the new DRM lines are continued past the M 03 point until they cross the path of the T—R line. Remember that the T—R line represents your ship's course and speed. The points at which the new DRM lines intersect the T—R line tell you the speed your ship would have to make in order to pass the target along that particular line. For instance, if you follow the new DRM line from where it crosses ahead of you, back into the plot, you see that it crosses the T—R line at about the 15 knot level. This tells you that if you were to slow your vessel to 15 knots, represented by moving R to that point, the target would move from the M 03 point along the new DRM line, passing you one mile ahead.

22

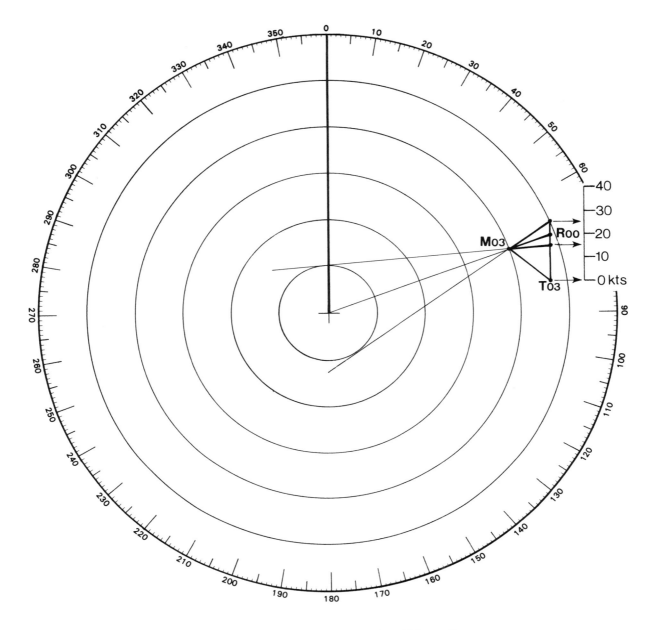

Figure 26. What speed must you make to pass the target one ring ahead? Astern?

Similarly, to pass the target one mile astern, follow that DRM line back through M to where it crosses the T—R line. Here, you have to make the T—R line longer because this maneuver requires a speed increase. The new DRM line crosses the T—R line at about the 25-knot level indicating that if, at time 03 you increase speed to 25 knots, you would pass this target one mile astern.

In the real world, however, your decision as to where to have the target pass you is largely dependent upon your vessel's speed and maneuvering capablity. For instance, if you wish the target in Figure 26 to pass astern, you must be able to increase speed so as to move the relative motion downscope. Remember—the DRM rules will always tell you what the target's track line will do in response to your chosen action.

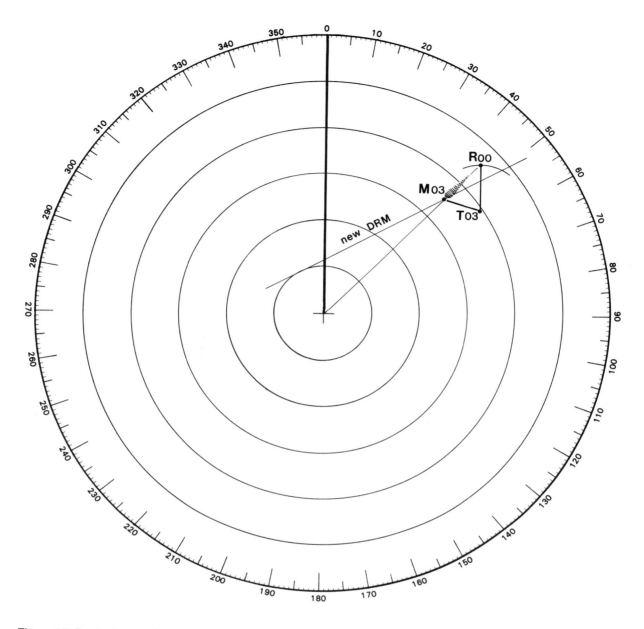

Figure 27. Beginning plot for a course change to the right.

COURSE CHANGE

The process of plotting a course change is almost identical to that of plotting a speed change. You still need to ask the basic questions which are "what is happening?" and "what is it you want to have happen?"

Consider the situation in Figure 27. A target which was plotted at time 00 and 03, bearing 45°, is seen to be closing on collision course. The "what is happening?" is obvious. A normal reaction would be to decide to turn to the right and pass the target, say, a mile off. You're on the six-mile range so that would be one range ring. How would the DRM change if you were to turn to the right? It is obviously a down target, and so the DRM will change to the right, or clockwise, in response to your right turn and thus, pass ahead of you and down your port side.

Complete the plot, placing R, T, and M as shown. Assume that you decide to maneuver at time 03 and that you intend to have the target pass ahead of you at one mile. Draw the clearance line, the new DRM

24

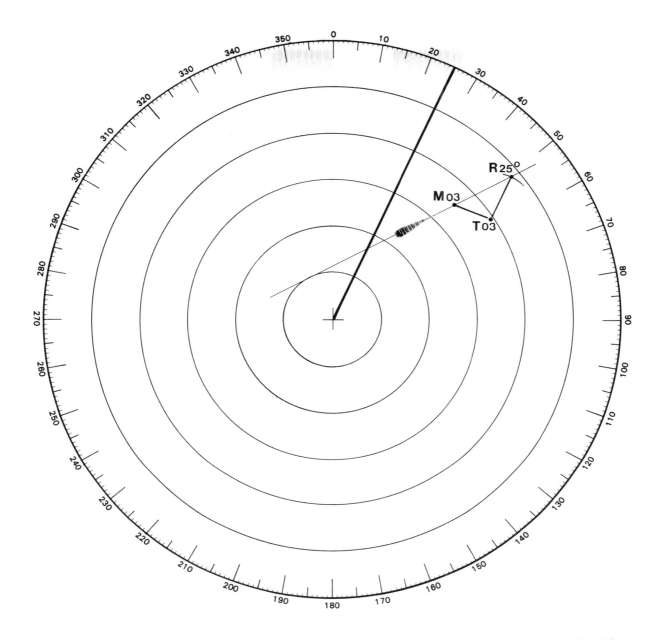

Figure 28. Completed right turn plot. Headflash is parallel to the new T—R line. The target will follow the new R—M line.

line, from the target's location at 03 to where you want the target to go. Now, bring that line back from point 03, through the plot, and out the back side, crossing the T—R line just as you did for a speed change. This time, though, you will continue past the T—R line as shown. Now, imagine yourself grabbing hold of Point R and pivoting around T as though it were a hinge. Swing the entire T—R line to the right, around T, until R falls on the new DRM line. A small arc of line is shown in Figure 27 to demonstrate how this plot would look if you used a compass or divider to determine this point.

Once R is placed on the new DRM line, you have only to read the new direction of T—R, often referred to as T—Rc (the new heading of your ship as a result of the (c)ourse change). T—Rc now points to the right of your original course of north, and the new R—M line (actually the Rc—M line) now indicates that the target will clear you by one range ring ahead as shown in Figure 28.

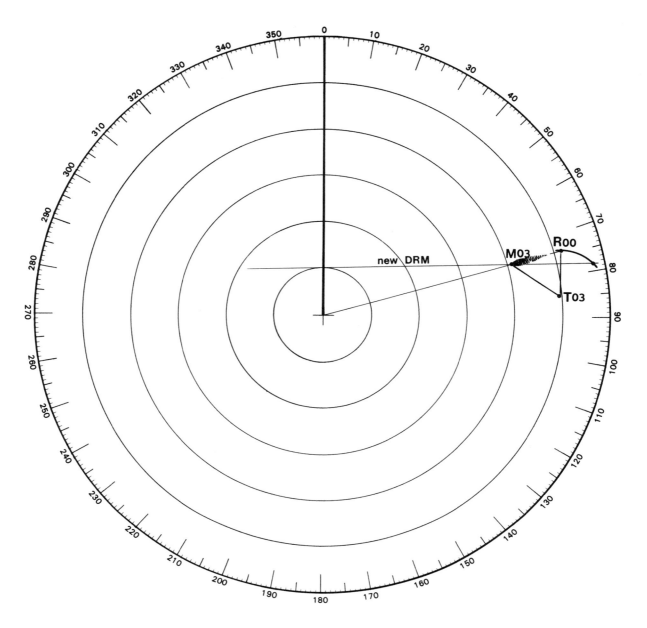

Figure 29. Beginning plot for a course change to the right.

What heading would you turn to? What direction is your headflash, the T—R line, now pointing? Check it against the bearing scale by laying the PGC (parallel grid cursor) parallel to the T—Rc line you just constructed. It comes out to about 25°. Now you can say that if, at time 03, you turned from north to a new heading of 25°, you would pass the threatening target one mile ahead along the new DRM line. Note also that when you know the direction or speed value of a new T—R line, it is very handy to mark the new known value at R. Here, Rc becomes R25°.

Try one more plot for practice. Figure 29 shows a target to starboard on collision course. This is a downscope target and a right turn will dispose of it easily, as the DRM will also change to the right or clockwise, passing the target ahead.

26

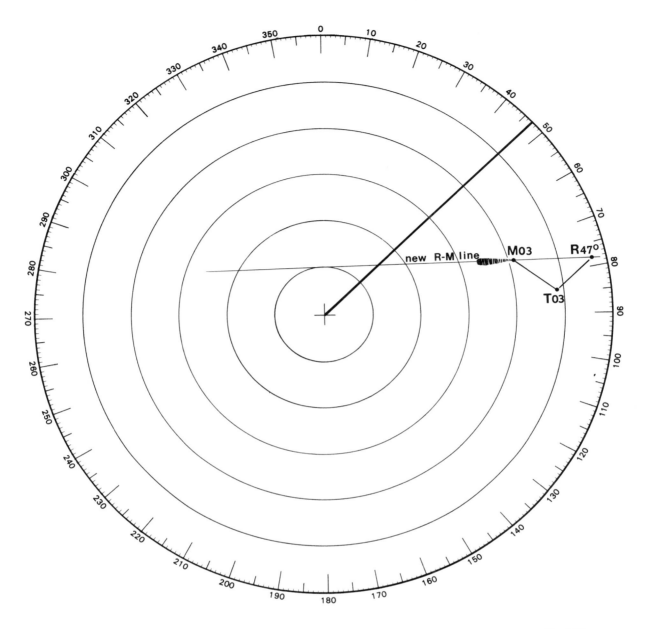

Figure 30. Completed right turn plot showing new heading (T—R line). The target is following the new R—M line.

The new DRM line indicating where you wish the target to pass is drawn from the point 03 since you plan to maneuver at that time. The line passes one ring ahead of your ship and is also extended back through the plot. Now, mentally grab ahold of Point R and pivot it around T to the right, dragging the original DRM line along as it "slides" through M. As you swing right, the DRM line also swings to the right until you have the plot as seen in Figure 30. The T—R line and your headflash are pointing to 47° and the relative motion line now appears between the new R and the original M to give you a CPA of one mile ahead.

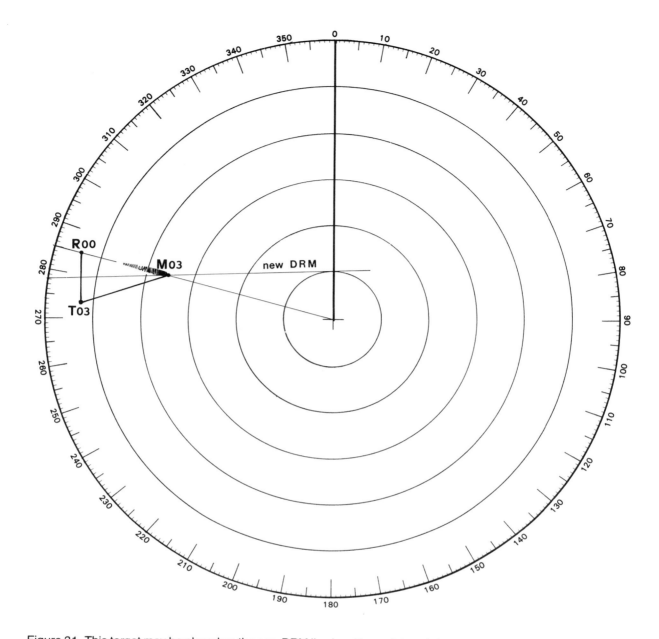

Figure 31. This target may be placed on the new DRM line by *either* a right or left turn.

There are some situations in which you have the choice of either a right or left turn. For instance, in Figure 31, you plot a new DRM line to pass one mile ahead. R may pivot around T either to the right or left, meeting the new DRM line in *two* places (Figure 32). Remembering that T—R shows the new heading of your ship, you may read your choice of new courses to steer between these points as shown. You could pass the target one mile ahead by coming either to 60° or to 296°. Note that there is a great difference in the

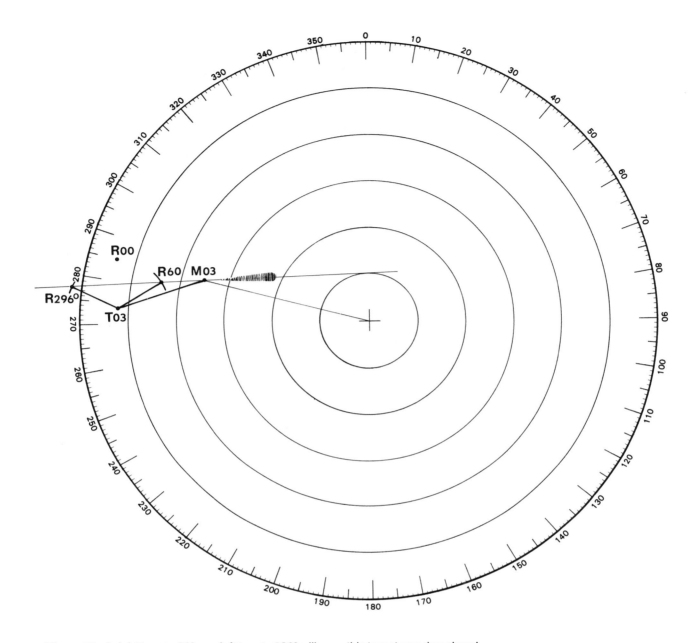

Figure 32. A right turn to 60° or a left turn to 296° will pass this target one ring ahead.

speeds of relative motion, depending upon your choice of maneuver. This should be taken into consideration along with other factors when planning your maneuver. Turning to 296° results in a large SRM while turning to 60° results in a very much slower SRM. Your choice of maneuver might well depend upon the length of time you are willing to spend getting rid of this particular contact.

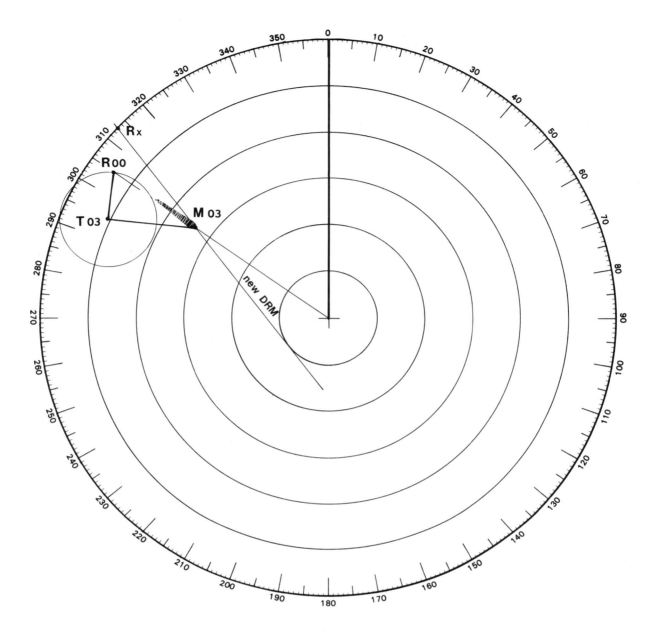

Figure 33. You cannot find any course to steer at 20 knots which will put this target astern!

One final example of the information you can gain from the plot. Suppose you decide to turn so as to put the target astern of your ship (see Figure 33). Draw the new DRM line from Point 03 to pass your ship one mile astern. Now, swing R around T as much as you want, even in a full circle as shown. Nowhere does the T—R line, or Point R, intersect the new DRM line. This simply tells you that your ship hasn't the speed to put the target ship astern. A quick check of the T—M line shows why: the other vessel is almost twice as fast as your ship. Notice, however, that if you were to increase your ship's speed by moving R up to the point marked Rx, you would, in fact put the target onto the new DRM line. Check it with your speed scale, T to Rx, and you will find that the required speed is about 39 knots.

5. "Real Time" Maneuvers

Up to this point, all maneuvering calculations have been made on the assumption (1) that you are able to make and implement your maneuvering decision instantaneously and (2) that your ship will turn or change speed instantly as well. This is, of course, possible only on paper. In order to plot and execute a maneuver in "real time," as with an actual ship, a slight modification of technique is necessary.

For instance, if you plot the target in Figure 34 just as before to give a one-ring clearance ahead, you will get a new T—R solution of 19°. This time, however, the target will not wait for you. After you close the plot at time 03, the target will continue to track toward you while you make your plot calculation. Suppose you took three minutes to place the new DRM line on the radarscope, back it up through the plot, and swing and read the new T—R line. By the time you establish your new course to steer, the target will be at Point 06. Now, allow two additional minutes for your ship to come to the new heading, and the target is at Point 08. As a result of this delay, *nothing* will happen to change the DRM of the target until time 08 and instead of clearing you by one ring, the target will track parallel to the line you plotted, but well inside it.

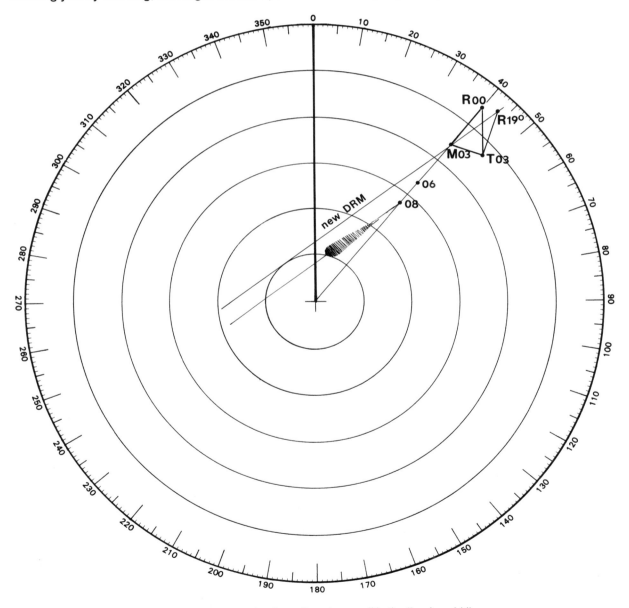

Figure 34. An instantaneous course change plot doesn't work so well in the "real world."

Correcting for this time lag is quite simple and requires only a small change in your technique. Figure 35 shows the same basic situation but allows for the additional time that will be needed for you to complete your plot, read the new heading, and bring your ship onto the new course. This time you will assume that all this will take a maximum of five minutes and that you will have completed all these steps on or before time 08. Quickly calculate where the target would be if you delayed until time 08 and draw a new DRM line (or clearance line) from that point to where you want the target to go; in this case a mile ahead. Parallel this new DRM line into the plot *through Point M*. Now, grasping R as if it were the end of a tiller, swing it to the right, pivoting on T, until it falls onto the new DRM line that passes through M. This point is now Rc and if you measure the direction of the T—Rc line you see it is 28°.

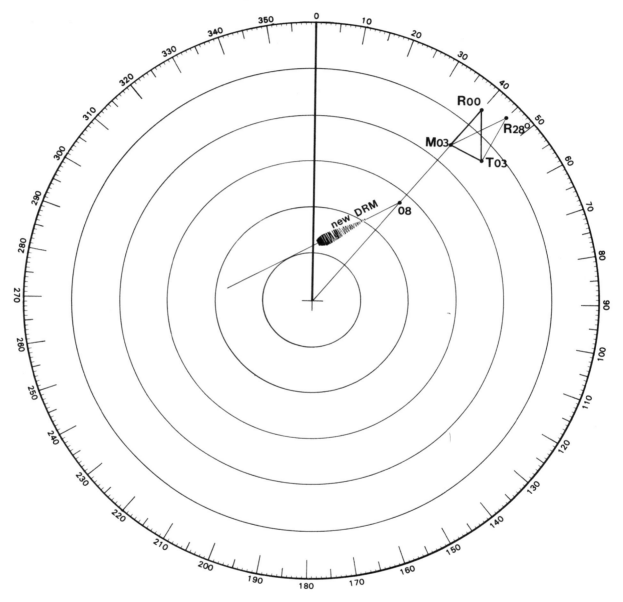

Figure 35. This delayed action plot allows for the time needed for thinking and maneuvering.

This, then, tells you that if you change to a new heading of 28° and complete the turn just as the target reaches Point 08, it will track exactly along the new DRM line and give you exactly a one-ring CPA. Unfortunately, that's a very big "if."

32

It is virtually impossible to plot and begin your maneuver so precisely that the target will follow the new DRM line exactly. In a real situation at sea, it won't matter whether you get a CPA of 0.8 miles or 1.3 miles instead of the 1.0 that you have plotted. There is, however, a very nice technique which will allow you to maneuver with "uncanny accuracy" every time.

Refer again to Figure 35, and assume that you pick Point 08 as your departure point. Make exactly the same plot as before but as soon as you have calculated the new course to steer: *Do it!* Begin the turn immediately. It certainly won't take three minutes to find the new heading, and thus you will be turning early. Your ship will come to the new heading of 28° *before* the target gets to Point 08. Now, the CPA will be greater than one ring by some amount. What remains is to return to the original heading at the right moment.

The final step is to place the PGC (parallel grid cursor) on the original relative motion line. Referring to Figure 36, you see the target which was tracking at "A" approach the grid line at "B." Ideally, you would like it to track down that first grid line, touching the one-mile ring. As the target approaches the line, about a quarter of a ring away, return your vessel to its original heading. The track will bend as shown at B and pass

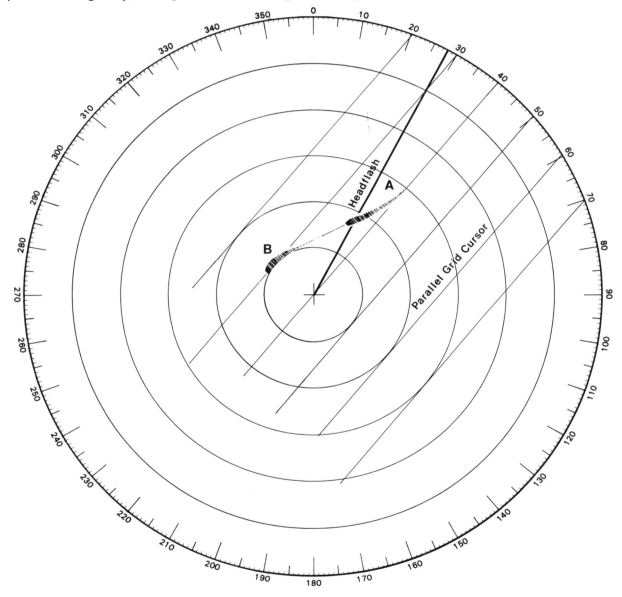

Figure 36. Use of the parallel grid cursor to indicate when to return to course.

exactly one mile off. The track does this because as you returned to your original course, the target returns to its original DRM. The PGC may be used in this manner to determine the "return point" for any maneuver, either course or speed change, as well as any combination of the two. The only tricky part is knowing how long your vessel takes to return to its original course and/or speed.

Now, in case you are having one of those days when everything seems to go wrong, you'll undoubtedly find that at least one of your plots just won't work. In Figure 37, the target has just passed Point 08 (Letter A) and is obviously not going to clear your ship by one ring. You probably won't have time to replot and so what you do is to eyeball the maneuver. Your original turn gives you some clearance but not enough. Therefore, you initiate an additional turn in the same direction so as to cause the target to increase the CPA that you have already gained (B). Once you have obtained a safe passing distance, it is only necessary to place the PGC on the original DRM line as before, and when the target approaches this line, as at C, return to your original course.

The most important thing here is to make certain that you obtain a one-ring CPA plus a small safety margin before cancelling the turn.

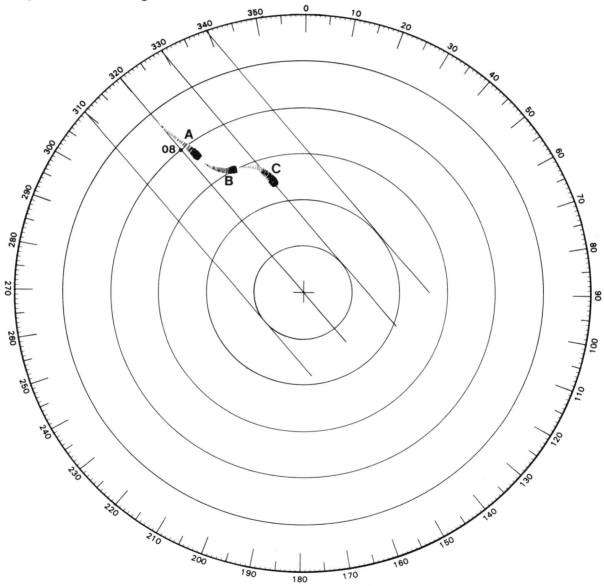

Figure 37. Secondary maneuver by eyeballing to achieve a one-ring CPA.

6. Target Vessel Maneuvers

While it's not likely that you would ever be called upon to plot a maneuver for another vessel, you may wish to be able to determine for yourself the effect of another ship's intended maneuver on the safety of your vessel. For instance, you might hear an announcement on the VHF to the effect that a vessel was intending to make some specific maneuver when abeam of a certain point. Or you might want to know what maneuver might be required to pass him a certain distance away from you. The plot is rather simple, requiring only the usual small modification of technique.

Refer to Figure 38. The plot shows a developing collision situation between your vessel and a portside target. In this situation, you will maintain course and speed while the target maneuvers to obtain a one-ring clearance astern.

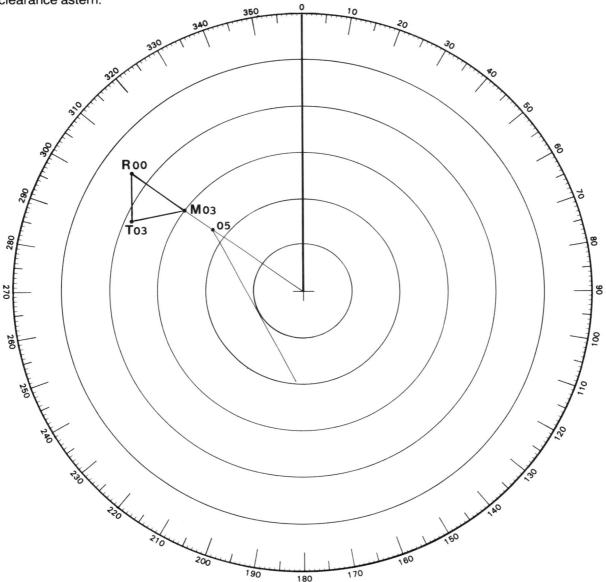

Figure 38. *Target* maneuver to avoid collision. Beginning plot.

Assume that you have plotted the situation as shown. What heading must the other vessel come to, maneuvering at time 05, to pass under your stern with a CPA of one mile? The initial plot and clearance line from Point 05 are exactly the same as if your vessel were going to maneuver. The difference comes in placing the new R—M line into the plot.

For your own vessel's maneuver, you have been placing the new R—M line into the plot through Point M. This was to allow Point R freedom to move. Now, however, Point R will remain fixed while Point M must be free to move. Thus, in this plot, *you will place the new R—M line into the plot through Point R.* Figure 39 shows this clearly: the new R—M line lies parallel to the clearance line extending from Point 05 and passes through Point Roo. The final step of the plot is to move M, relative to T, to intersect the new DRM line. The other vessel will make a right turn to pass under your stern so that Point M, pivoting on T, will swing to the right until it falls onto the new R—M line at Point Mc. The heading indicated by line T—Mc is about 133° and is the new heading the other vessel must steer in order to attain the indicated CPA.

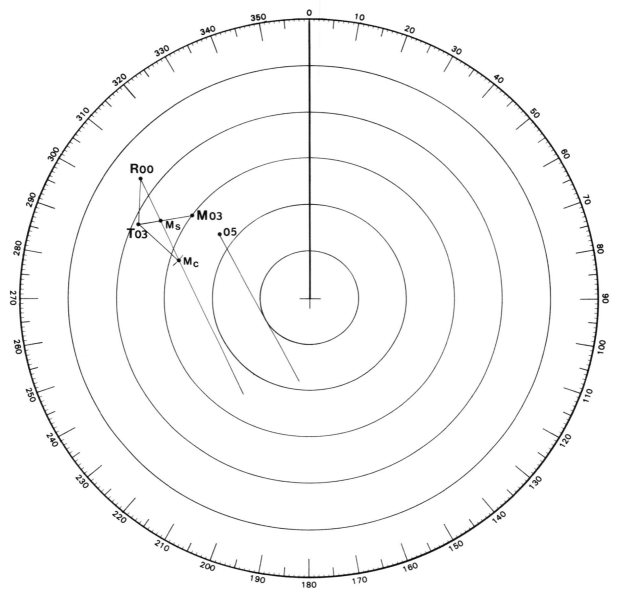

Figure 39. *Target* maneuver to avoid collision. Completed plot.

You may also derive the amount of speed reduction the other vessel would have to make in order to accomplish the same CPA. Look again at Figure 39. The point at which the new DRM line intersects the T—M line, marked Ms, indicates the speed change necessary to accomplish this maneuver. If you measure it, you will find that a reduction to about 9 knots (T—Ms) from the original speed of 22 knots (T—M03) will do the trick.

This leads to another one of those off-the-wall rules:

If *our* ship is to maneuver, maneuver with the letter "*R*".

To maneuver *him* (the other vessel), maneuver with "*M*".

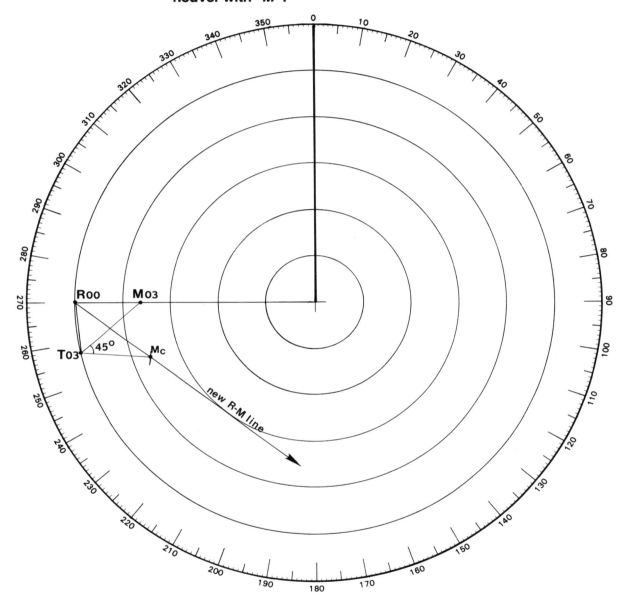

Figure 40. The target changes course 45° to the right.

Try one more of these before moving on. Suppose, in Figure 40, the target were to turn 45° to the right at time 05, what would the new CPA be? To answer this, you first have to decide what is going to happen within the basic plot. The line T—R is not going to change; your ship will maintain course and speed. The target vessel will maneuver and that means you are going to do something with Point M. What are you going to do? Well, since the vessel is going to turn 45° to the right, you have to ask "to the right of what?" The answer is "to the right of its present course," and that is shown by the line T—M. In short, you will move the T—M line so that it points 45° to the right of its present heading, pivoting on T. That makes Point M swing down to the point marked Mc. T—Mc is the new course the other vessel will steer, and the line R—Mc shows you the value of the new DRM that you will observe on the scope after the maneuver. Now, what will the new CPA be after the target changes course?

OK, all of you who said the new CPA would be three rings can spend the next watch down in the bilge looking for the golden rivet! The new CPA will *not* be three rings at all because you didn't take into account one very important fact about a target's plotted maneuver. In this plot, your new DRM line always winds up somewhere off the actual track of the target. The DRM value or direction is correct. It merely doesn't connect with the target's previous track.

Look again at Figure 40, remembering that the target maneuver was to occur at time 05. *Where was the target at time 05?* Figure 40 has not yet made any reference to the 05 point. In Figure 41, the new DRM

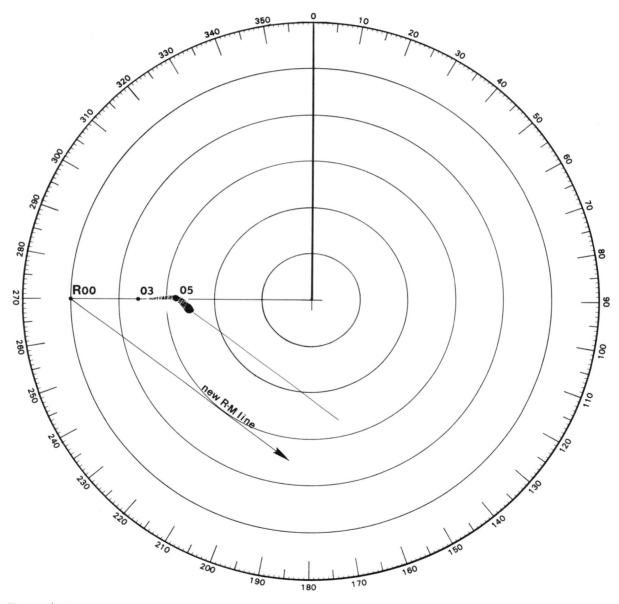

Figure 41. The new CPA is 1¾ miles.

38

line plotted in the previous figure has been moved out to the 05 point. This is the track that the target ship will actually follow on your radar. The new CPA will be a bit less than two rings.

The error just demonstrated is very common since it is easy to forget that there are basic differences between maneuvering your own ship and doing what looks like the same thing with the other vessel. Always remember to place the new relative motion line at the place *where* and *when* the action actually takes place.

7. Advanced Techniques

The term "advanced techniques" is deceptive. Ordinarily, it might mean that what is to follow is going to be very complicated. However, having advanced as a student you should find the following to be both simple and useful.

THE HALF-ANGLE RULE

The half-angle rule applies only to targets which are on the same course and speed as your vessel.

The first part of the rule states that if you plan a specific course change, by placing the right-angle mark of your PGC halfway between your present heading and your intended heading, the body of the PGC will indicate the new DRM of any target on the same course and speed.

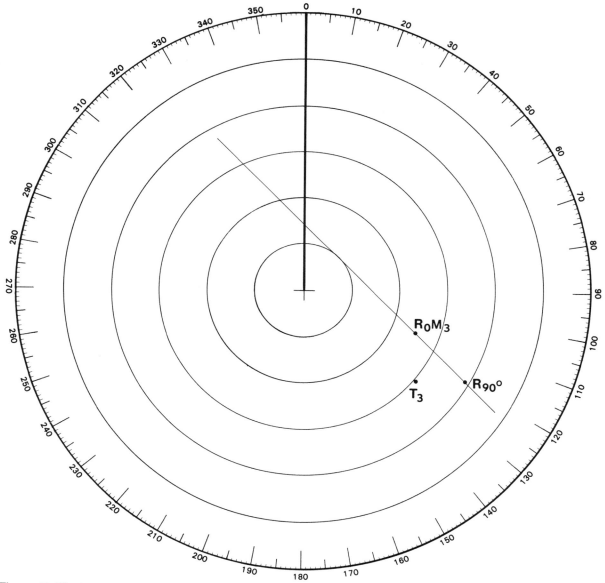

Figure 42. The target vessel is on the same course and speed as your ship. Plot to pass it one ring ahead by turning right.

40

The second part states that if you desire a specfic CPA with a target presently on the same course and speed, you may find the new course to steer by first placing the PGC so as to indicate an appropriate passing distance ahead or astern, then reading the position of the right-angle index to the PGC body. This index is now indicating *half* of the total course change necessary to achieve your intended CPA. *Double* this value, and you have the course to steer.

Figure 42 demonstrates a standard R—T—M plot to pass a same course and speed target one ring ahead. Now, in order to make this explanation somewhat plausible, assume (1) that you have no engine maneuvers available, (2) that you really do want to turn to the right, and finally (3) that a left turn is totally out of the question. In other words, you *are* going to make a turn to the right, the only question is how to do it without risking a collision or giving the other skipper heart failure. Your plot indicates that if you change course 90° to the right, to 090°T, you will pass the target on the starboard safely one ring ahead.

The same result may be obtained by using the PGC (Figure 43). You wish to pass the target one ring ahead of your ship. Place the grid so that it marks a line from the target to a point one ring ahead of your ship. The right-angle line now points to 45°, and since you are using the *half-angle rule,* you will *double* this value to obtain a course to steer of 090°T.

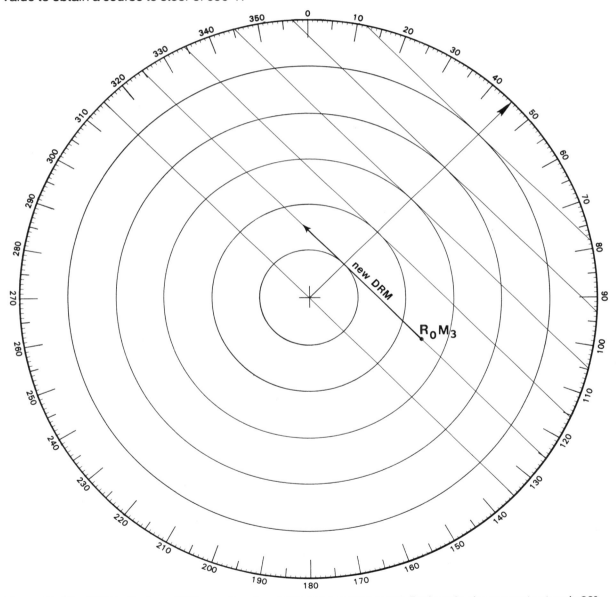

Figure 43. The PGC indicates a CPA one ring ahead. The index points to 45°. By the rule, the course to steer is 90°.

Try one more for practice. In Figure 44, a target is located on the second ring, abaft your starboard beam. You wish to turn right to 45°. Will this put your ship into danger?

To find out, set the right-angle index on your PGC to *half* of your total turn or 22½°. The body of the PGC now shows you the new DRM of the target and predicts a collision situation.

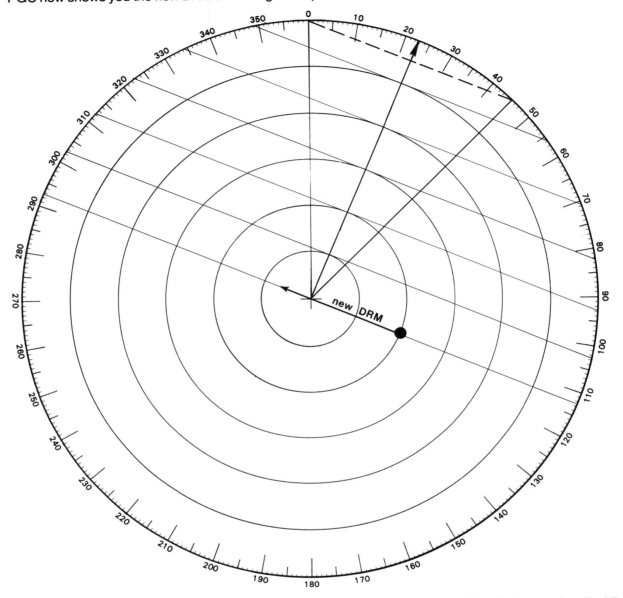

Figure 44. The new DRM of a same course and speed target may be plotted using the "old headflash—new headflash" technique.

Note also, that you can perform the same calculation without using the PGC. In Figure 44, you see a dashed line connecting your original heading, 000°, and your new heading, 045°. This line, parallel to the cursor in the half-angle configuration, may be used as an accurate indication of the new DRM, and is the same as the new R—M line you would obtain if you were to plot the change using the full R—T—M triangle or the half-angle rule. Should your radar lack an adequate PGC or if the PGC is broken, this method of establishing the new DRM of a same course and speed target is equally as accurate.

You may also use the half-angle rule to determine the limits of an intended maneuver. Figure 45 shows a target, again on the starboard quarter and on the same course and speed as your vessel. You wish to pass this target either one ring astern or one ring ahead by turning right.

42

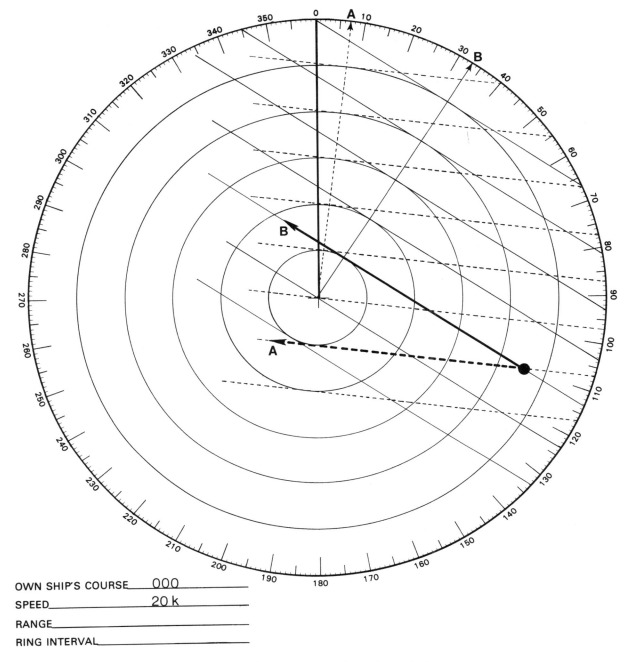

OWN SHIP'S COURSE ___000___
SPEED ___20 k___
RANGE _____
RING INTERVAL _____

Figure 45. Turning to 14° puts this target one ring astern; to 66°, one ring ahead.

Beginning with the right-angle index of the PGC on your heading of 000°, rotate it slowly to the right until one of the "one-ring" lines of the PGC falls directly onto the target. This setting of the PGC is marked with dots, and the track that the target would follow is marked with heavy dots. This line passes the target one ring astern along line A, an acceptable CPA according to your night orders. Your course to steer may be determined from the right-angle index, letter A, which is indicating 007°. Since you are using the half-angle rule, your course to steer is actually 014°.

You probably have already seen that there is a problem with this maneuver. Your speed of relative motion is very low, and it will take quite a long time to disengage from this target. A second solution exists, however, if you should choose to pass the target ahead of your ship.

To determine your course to steer in order to pass the target one ring ahead, continue turning the PGC to the right until again the "one-ring" line rests over the target. This time, however, the line passes the

43

target ahead of your ship. This position is shown in solid lines. The target will pass you along line B. The right-angle index points to 033°, Point B, and again, since you are using the half-angle rule, you must double this value to 066° in order to obtain the course to steer. In this case, the speed of relative motion will be much greater than in case A, and you should be able to bring the other vessel to CPA in a much shorter time.

Now you have established the limits of your maneuver, based upon a minimum one-ring CPA. Any turn between 000° and 014° is acceptable. Between 014° and 066° will create a CPA of less than one ring. Any turn greater than 066° will again result in a one-ring or better clearance.

Try plotting these maneuvers using both the normal R—T—M plot as well as the original headflash—new headflash technique. You will see that all three methods give the same result.

MULTIPLE TARGET PROBLEMS

Sooner or later, you will find yourself in a real jackpot situation. Perhaps it will seem that all the ships in the world have decided to appear on the radar at one time—and it *had* to be on your watch! All is not lost, however. The DRM rules will prove most useful here and what the DRM rules won't handle, you and your plotting skills will! Take a look at Figure 46.

Four targets, A, B, C, and D are shown on the six-mile range. A and C are on collision course and therefore represent your most immediate threats. B is dead astern on the same course and speed as your ship. D is ahead to port and has apparently taken one look at the mess you are a part of and is wisely maneuvering to get clear. You probably can ignore him for the next few minutes while you concentrate on the other three.

Target B prevents you from reducing speed. You never want to turn toward a limbo target abeam at close range, Target C, and so your best bet is a right turn. This will increase the SRM of Target A while decreasing that of B, making A your most critical target, the one which will threaten your vessel first. Thus, the first plot will be made on Target A.

Allowing three minutes for plotting and maneuvering, plot an avoidance course change to the right so as to pass Target A one ring ahead. Your course to steer comes out to be about 35° to the right or 035° true. Will this course change get you clear of all the other targets? To find out, apply the following rule:

That which thou doest unto the one, go
and do thou likewise unto all the rest, in
full and equal measure.
—The Book of Samuel (VW)

If Noah had radar aboard the ark, it's certain he would have used this rule. Basically, it states that whatever maneuver you plan in order to avoid one target must be applied equally to all other targets on your plot, both in the amount and direction of maneuver and in the time of execution. Your plot solution for Target A gives a right turn to 35°, and you plan to do this by time 06. Therefore, you must plot a 35° course change at time 06 against all other targets which are liable to be dangerous—in this case, Targets B and C.

Target B is on the same course and speed as you are, and a quick check with the PGC shows it will pass clear under your stern. Using the half-angle rule, set the right-angle index to 17½°. The grid body now shows you the new DRM. Alternatively, you may plot as shown.

Target C shows a new DRM of about 335° which, stepped ahead to the 06 position, indicates that it, too, will pass well clear. The DRM rules indicate that Target D will continue to open range. Thus, you may conclude that the maneuver will be safe and effective.

To review: Using the DRM rules, you estimated risk of collision for each target. For the one which presented the most immediate threat, you plotted an avoidance maneuver. Then, by two different means, the RTM plot and the half-angle rule, you assessed future risk of collision in regard to the other targets in the vicinity. Now look at Figure 47, and try one more.

Of the five targets shown, only D presents an immediate threat. Suppose you wish to make a navigational course change to 42°. Can you do so and still maintain a one-ring clearance on all traffic?

44

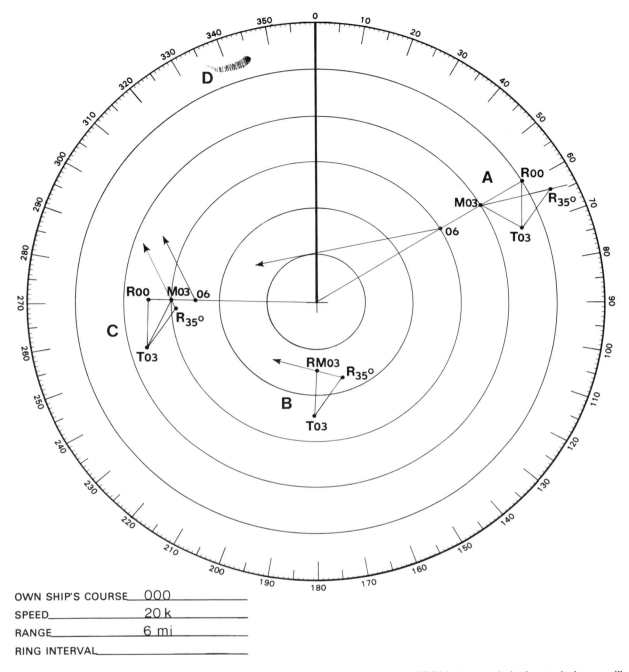

OWN SHIP'S COURSE 000
SPEED 20 k
RANGE 6 mi
RING INTERVAL

Figure 46. Multiple target situations appear complex but proper application of DRM rules and plotting techniques will help.

First, find which targets do not and will not threaten your ship. E appears to be the only one. B and C may be easily plotted if you recognize and understand their special characteristics. B is DIW (dead-in-the-water). You know that a DIW will always track parallel to your course (headflash) and in the opposite direction. Thus, if you plan to turn to 42°, B will track a new DRM of 222°. Depending on when you make your course change, you could be in trouble. Anytime before 09 brings you into less than a one-ring CPA. After time 09, a 42° change right is OK.

What about Target C? That one is same course and speed on your starboard quarter. This is a maneuver that has to be carefully worked out. You do it this time: use your PGC and the half-angle rule. The plot has been worked out so you can check your results. Set the right-angle line to *half* of the total turn, 21°.

45

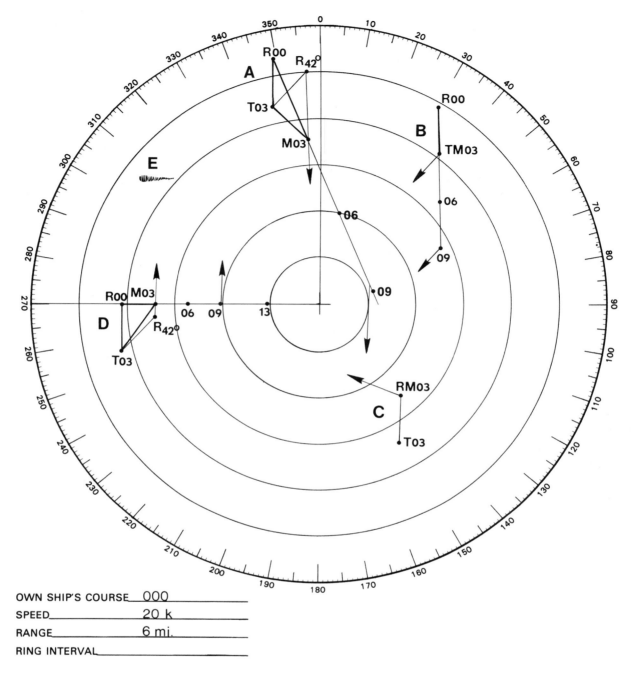

OWN SHIP'S COURSE 000
SPEED 20 k
RANGE 6 mi.
RING INTERVAL

Figure 47. Two targets in this multiple situation present little or no threat.

The body of the grid now shows you the new DRM of Target C and you can see that it will pass well clear under your stern. Time of maneuver is not a factor here since this target isn't going anywhere until you do something.

Target D is on collision course, in limbo and closing at a moderate speed. A change to 042° will send the DRM zooming upscope. As long as the change is made before time 13, there will be no problem.

Things are indeed becoming a bit tight! You can't maneuver before time 09 and must maneuver before time 13. And, there's still one more target to consider.

Target A is presently passing well clear to starboard. A right turn to 042°, however, will bring A inside the one-mile ring if done anytime before time 09. This is fine as you didn't really want to turn before that time anyway because of Target B.

To sum up, what are your options regarding a right turn to 042°? Before time 09, you are in conflict with Targets A and B. After time 13, Target D gets too close. Between times 09 and 13, you are safe to turn to 042° and will clear all targets by one ring or more.

You should notice that there are several potential solutions to these situations. The problem in Figure 47 responds nicely to a speed reduction as well as a course change right, if collision avoidance is your only goal. In these and other similar multiship problems, there is seldom a single "correct" solution as opposed to "incorrect" solutions. Many factors, in addition to the plot, must enter into your ultimate decision: the Rules of the Road, inability to change speed at short notice, maneuverability and, of course, your schedule. Generally, your ability to make the correct decision will continue to grow and improve with experience and *practice*.

THE HALF-STANDARD PLOT

The more advanced student may also be able to profit from another technique developed to assist with "emergency" plotting. The half-standard plot will give you needed information in half the time needed for the full time plot. It is accomplished easily by cutting your standard plot period in half. For instance, on the 24-mile range, a 6-minute plot is performed. On the 3-mile range, a 45-second plot will suffice. As you can see, the plot time becomes a quarter of the range scale in use, in minutes.

The half-standard plot has one advantage: If you need the plot and maneuvering data in a hurry, you obtain it twice as fast using this method. On the other hand, the disadvantages must be considered as well. Using the half-standard plot, your accuracy is greatly reduced since your line lengths are half what they would be in standard time. It can become a finicky exercise in fine drafting technique which, coupled with ship motion and vibration, can lead to substantial errors.

You should be aware of the time advantage to be obtained from using this type of plot and be able to balance these advantages against its obvious limitations. If you ever contemplate using this method, it would be wise to practice it under nonthreatening conditions in conjunction with the standard plot. In this manner, you can observe the type and magnitude of errors that occur and perhaps, take steps to reduce them.

8. Relative Motion Modes

While much has been written on the various uses of radar, relatively little, outside of the technical manuals, has appeared describing the various modes of presentation. True motion has been described rather completely, but relative motion has only been covered in terms of north-stabilized operation. There are three additional relative motion modes that should be considered.

Early in the book, a statement was made that the mode of radar operation to be used was stabilized relative motion. This designation should have been north-stabilized relative motion because, in fact, this has been the only form of relative motion described. In all discussions, north has been at the top of the scope while your own ship's heading has been indicated by the headflash line pointing to the true compass direction.

Unstabilized, or ship's head up radar has been in use since the earliest days of RAdio Detection And Ranging. Of course, the first radar was not aboard a moving ship but was developed ashore where the question of relative motion versus true motion and the effects of yaw, set, and drift were problems that never arose.

As soon as radar was mounted upon a moving platform, the difficulties began. Small alterations in direction induced by yaw as well as larger variations occasioned by collision avoidance maneuvering or navigational course changes all resulted in a broken or discontinuous radar track. To obtain a correct value of DRM and CPA in order to assess risk of collision, it became necessary to construct a "transfer" or paper plot which would eliminate the effects of yaw or course changes, and present the observer with an azimuth-stabilized picture. Figure 48 shows an unstabilized radar and a collision course target. Yawing of the observer's ship results in a skewing of the relative motion line. If an "average" of this motion were taken, it would probably predict a close quarter situation, if not collision. However, depending upon when the watch officer reads the radar screen, it might just as easily predict a one-ring CPA to either port or starboard!

A course change for collision avoidance purposes can be equally confusing in unstabilized relative motion. Figure 49 shows the same target reacting to a 45° course change to the right. As the target reaches 3.5 miles, a right turn to 045° is begun. Since your ship's heading indication cannot change, the headflash is fixed at 000° relative. The entire radar picture must then rotate *counter* to the direction of your turn or to the left. The target winds up bearing about 340° relative, and as you watch the picture develop, you still don't have much of an idea as to whether or not it's going to pass clear. As a matter of fact, the target will pass clear at about one mile down your port side. In order to establish this fact, however, you would have to make a transfer plot.

Azimuth-stabilized radar, most commonly used and referred to as north-stabilized radar, is coupled to a master compass or gyro in order to obtain a directional reference. If you were to rerun the situation in Figure 48 using this mode of presentation, we would obtain a picture as shown in Figure 50. The threatening target bearing 025° maintains a steady DRM track while the radar headflash, indicating the 10° yaw, wanders back and forth between 355° and 005°.

A turn to 045° at this point would cause the target image to react according to the DRM rules: as your headflash shifts right, the target's DRM track also shifts to its right or clockwise giving you an uninterrupted picture of the CPA, and thus, the change in the risk of collision remains quite apparent at all times.

North-stabilized radar is really a big help in maintaining a continual observation of your traffic and its relation to your ship—as long as your course is north or a heading not too far from it. The big objection comes when you are running, say, from Nova Scotia south to Cape Horn. On this heading, the headflash of a north-stabilized radar spends days pointing at your belt buckle. All down targets look like up targets and you are liable to get a crick in your neck from trying to look at the picture "from behind." Your best answer to this problem is to place the radar into "base course up" mode. In this configuration, your base course, let's

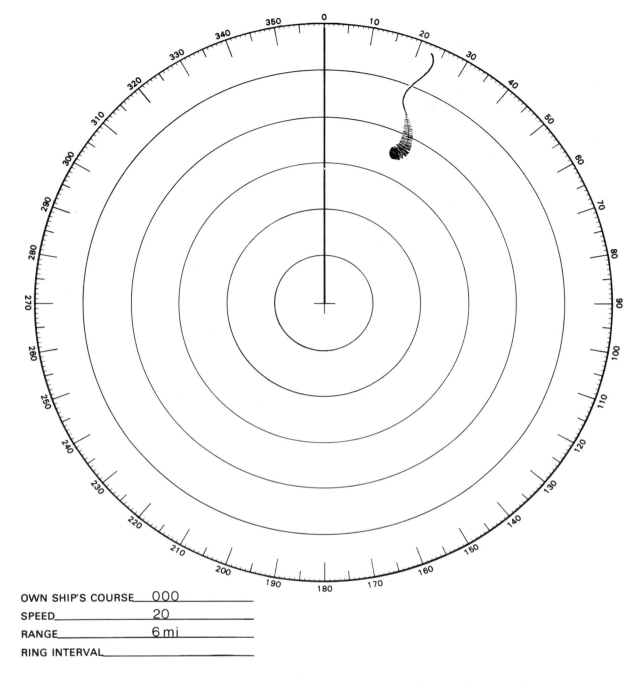

OWN SHIP'S COURSE 000

SPEED 20

RANGE 6 mi

RING INTERVAL

Figure 48. Unstabilized (ship's head up) radar showing the effect of yaw on a collision course target.

say, south, is placed at the top of the scope. On most radars this can be done by using the gyro repeater set control or the headflash manual alignment control—the one you ordinarily use to set the headflash to the true base course. Figure 51 shows your radar in BCUSRMM (base course up stabilized relative motion mode), course 180°, yaw 10°, total.

You should be able to see the major disadvantage of this display mode at a glance. Although your course is actually south, it looks like north. After all these years of looking at radar with north at the top, you

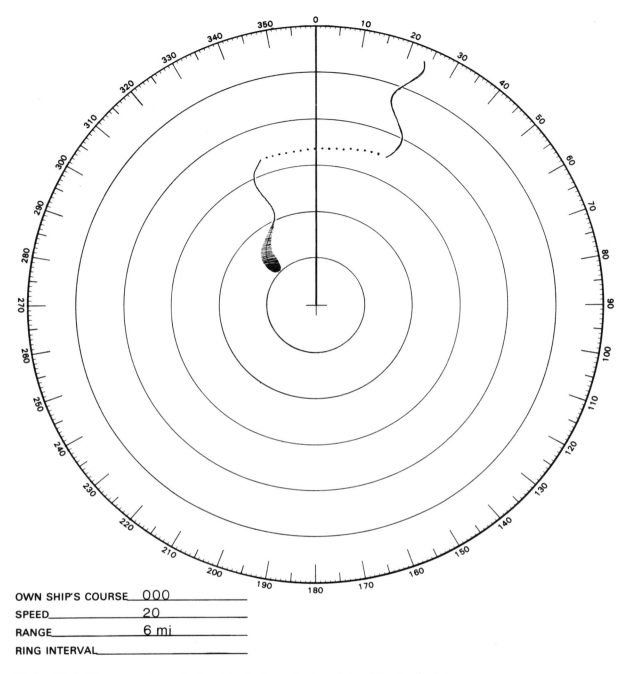

OWN SHIP'S COURSE___000_____
SPEED_____20_____
RANGE_____6 mi_____
RING INTERVAL_____

Figure 49. A 45° course change to the right displaces the target, breaking the track line.

could easily make some serious errors in reading both true and relative bearings. This problem is eased somewhat if your radar has an auxiliary bearing scale which is driven by the master gyro. In any case, you should be very careful in taking any bearings and translating them to true directional reference. *Finally, don't forget to tell your relief that the radar is set base course up!*

The final operational mode is often referred to as DSRM (double-stabilized relative motion). This mode requires too many hands waving in the air to describe graphically, and so allow your imagination to work overtime a bit. Look back at Figure 50. Your base course is north, and you wish to turn right to a new course of 045°. Ordinarily, the headflash would turn slowly to the right as you turn, winding up at the 045° position. Now, imagine that your radar is mounted on a turntable and is free to rotate any way you wish to

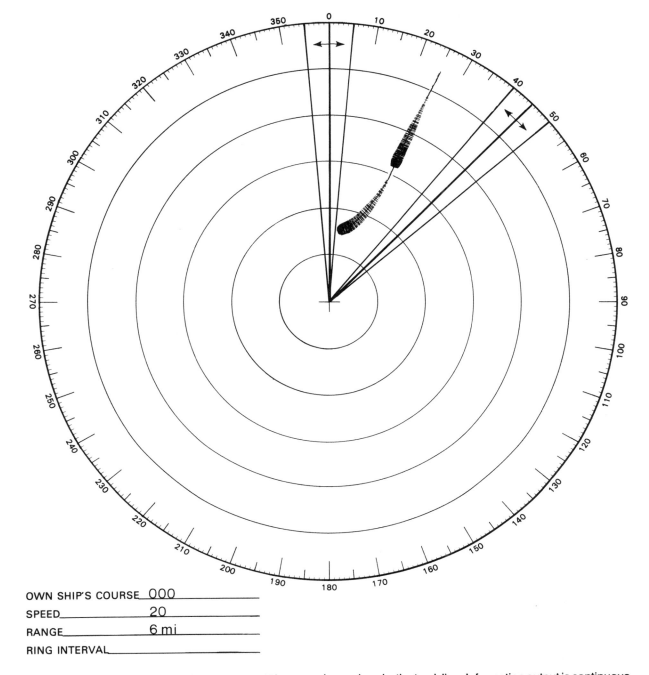

OWN SHIP'S COURSE __000__

SPEED __20__

RANGE __6 mi__

RING INTERVAL _____

Figure 50. Stabilized radar: neither yaw nor a 45° course change breaks the track line. Information output is continuous.

turn it. As the headflash moves that first degree, from 000° to 001°, you grab the display unit and rotate it one degree counterclockwise, thus putting the headflash back where you like it: straight up away from you. When the headflash moves the next degree to the right, rotate the display on its bearings to place it again at the exact top of the scope. Keep doing this until the headflash has reached the 045° position and stops moving. At this point, the headflash is still pointing directly away from you and is resting over the 045° reference mark which is now at the top of the scope. There has been no smearing or discontinuity in the target tracks on the screen because this is stabilized radar. You merely rotated the entire console to keep the headflash pointing away from you.

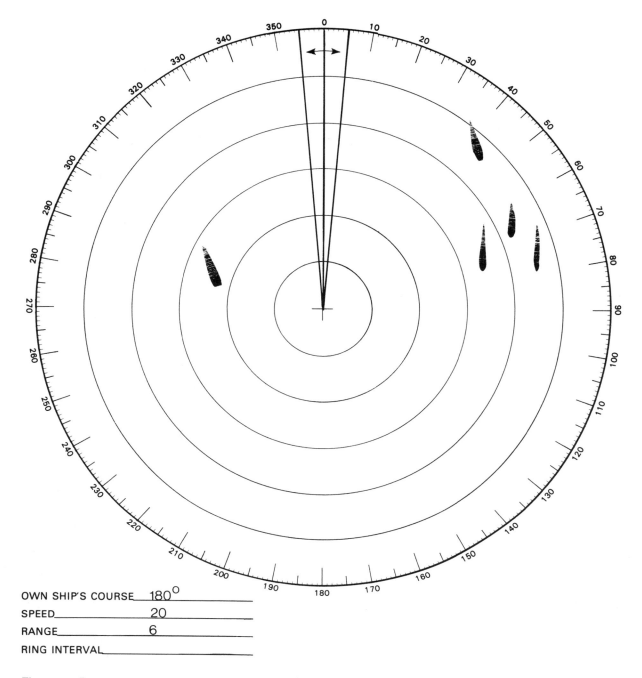

OWN SHIP'S COURSE ___180°___
SPEED ___20___
RANGE ___6___
RING INTERVAL _____

Figure 51. Base course (180°) up stabilized relative motion.

Of course, you could accomplish the same thing by walking around the display console, but this is usually impossible as radar cabinets are seldom mounted clear of all obstructions. In actual practice, the process of double stabilization is carried out either by mechanically rotating the azimuth display components inside the indicator console or by performing the task with some form of computer graphics. One of the best examples of this stabilization mode is found in the Kelvin-Hughes situation display. While there are relatively few double-stabilized units in use today, they will surely increase in proportion to the number of computer-generated radar displays being utilized.

True motion radar may also be used in the base course up mode and could be provided with double stabilization as well.

9. True Motion

In order to understand true motion, it is helpful to imagine that you are hovering over the ocean or a harbor in a helicopter and viewing the ships and land features. The vessels underway are seen to move in their proper direction and speed; the land, docks, and bridges, etc., are seen to be stationary. You could get the same effect if you were working with a maneuvering board, chart plot, or model table wherein all motions would be seen exactly in the direction and speed at which they were actually occurring. Figure 52 shows two vessels, one eastbound and one northbound. Depending upon their actual (or true) speeds, they will move across the picture in the direction of their heading, and assuming they do not collide, they will eventually pass off the edge of the frame.

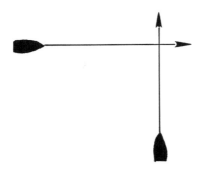

Figure 52. An overhead view of two ships showing true motion vectors.

This type of situation viewed on a true motion radar would appear as in Figure 53. The first thing you might notice is that the picture appears to be off center. This is correct and normal, and, in fact, when using true motion, you will find that the picture is almost never centered. Instead the picture may appear anywhere on the scope. The next "surprise" is that your ship's position at the center of the range rings is constantly moving, as long as you are underway, and takes the headflash, rings, and any other features such as the variable range ring or electronic bearing line along with it. If your radar makes a spot of light at the center of the display, then it will leave a tail behind it just as the targets have been doing in relative motion. This is because, of course, your ship's position is now moving across the radarscope in the direction of your headflash and at a speed proportional to your actual travel. (Initially, this discussion will ignore the effects of wind and current.) The tails appearing behind the targets and your vessel, then, give you an immediate appreciation of the true course and speed of all vessels, including your own!

Figure 53 shows three targets. To port is a vessel crossing your bow from west to east and making approximately the same speed as your vessel. Target speed is estimated by comparing the length of the observed tail to the tail left by your ship. On your starboard bow is a target showing no tail. That contact is not moving—it is dead in the water. On the starboard beam is a vessel on the same course and speed as yours. It is important to understand the difference these last two targets have in appearance in the true motion mode as compared with the relative motion mode. Simply stated, in each case, their appearances are reversed. And now, another word of caution: if you intend to use true and relative motion displays interchangeably, you must be able to shift your thinking quickly and accurately when assessing the nature of these two types of target!

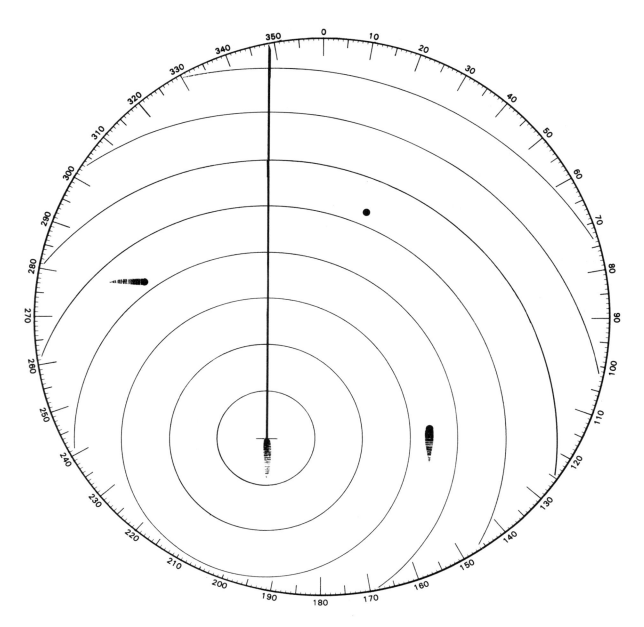

Figure 53. A true motion radar presentation.

REASONS FOR USING TRUE MOTION

True motion radar has two basic advantages over relative motion. The first is that it is capable of showing the true course and speed of the targets. Second, it displays stationary objects as being motionless on the radar screen and thus, buoys, landmasses, and harbor details do not smear on your display as they do in relative motion. Imagine yourself making an approach to a crowded, busy anchorage. Identifying buoys, anchored ships, and slow-moving vessels underway in relative motion, becomes an exercise in eyestrain. The same scene in true motion is almost ridiculously simple. The buoys and anchored vessels all appear as sharp, nonmoving points while the moving objects not only are obvious, but their tracks indicate their course and speed.

54

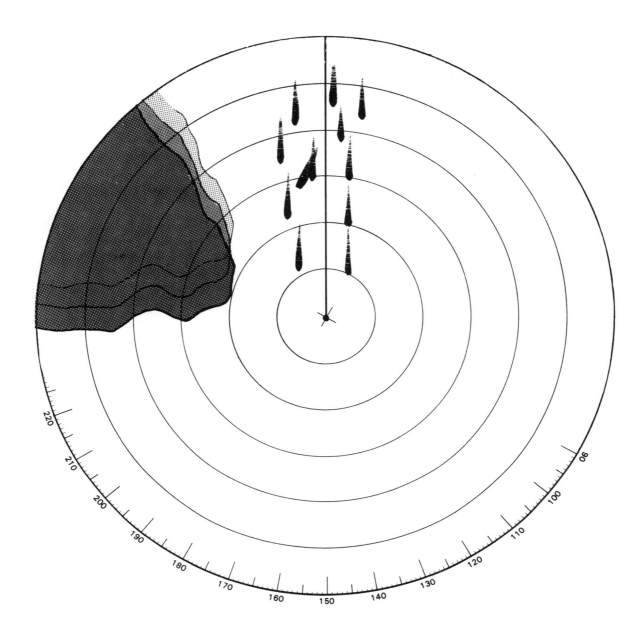

Figure 54. Land mass, traffic, and channel markers in *relative motion.*

Figures 54 and 55 show the same scene in both relative and true presentation. In the relative motion display, the point of land and the channel markers move toward your ship's position which is fixed in the center of the scope. As the picture starts to develop, the buoy tracks begin to cover each other and can actually mask the location of nearby objects. The landmass presents a large yellow smear that is distracting to the eye. Moving traffic about midway through the channel is difficult to detect.

The true motion display in Figure 55 is quite different. Landmasses and buoys are stationary while the traffic approaching your position is quite obvious. In general, the display is clean and easily understood when compared to the confusion in Figure 54.

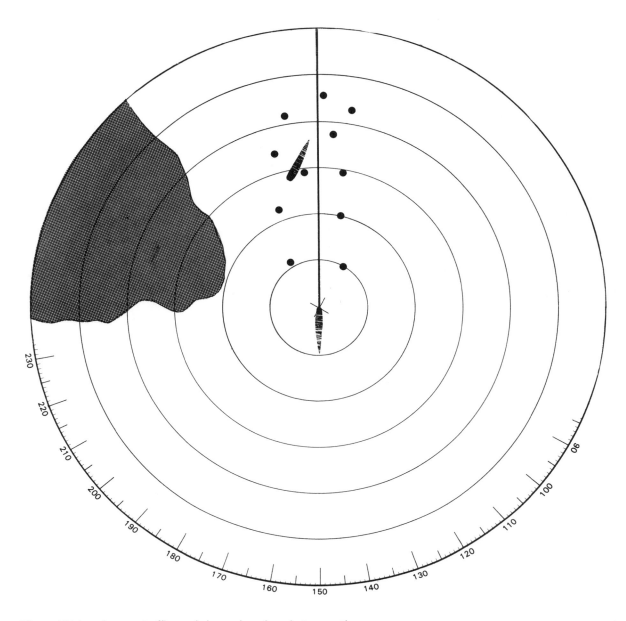

Figure 55. Land mass, traffic, and channel markers in *true motion*.

56

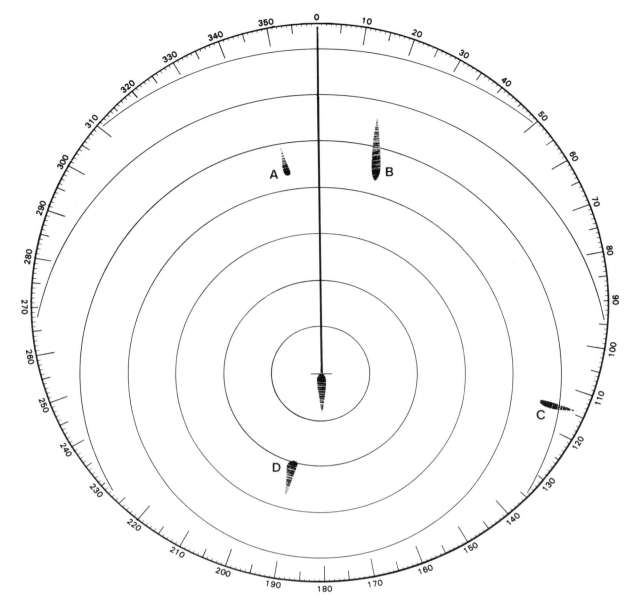

Figure 56. Risk of collision is often difficult to assess when using true motion.

After all that, true motion certainly sounds fine, doesn't it? Well it is, and it's very good at doing what it does best: making sense of situations in which there are a lot of stationary objects, and showing the true tracks of moving vessels. However, as stated at the beginning of this book, it does make collision avoidance a bit awkward. To assess the risk of collision, the relative motion of a target must be known, and this is the one thing that the true motion display does not offer. For this information you must plot!

Consider the situation in Figure 56 for a moment. Four targets appear on the six-mile range. With relative motion, you could predict a collision with Target D and close quarters with A and C. In true motion, however, only Target A presents a collision threat while B, C, and D will pass well clear. Target B shows an obvious clear passage in both modes as it is moving parallel to the headflash and thus, its relative motion track is very close to its true motion vector or its reciprocal. If you do not intend to plot for collision risk assessment, you should be very careful when selecting true motion in congested situations.

57

THE BASIC T—R—M PLOT

The T—R—M plot (No! That's not a misprint. It's meant to be read as "T—R—M.") begins by placing a dot over the target on the radarscope as in Figure 57 A. Label that dot Point T and mark the time, for instance, 00. Take a moment to make certain you understand the following procedure. In True motion you begin the plot with T. In Relative motion, the plot begins with R and that's a handy way to remember which comes first.

The geometry of the plot is exactly the same as before in that the three lines, T—R, T—M, and R—M, still designate your ship's course and speed, the course and speed of the target, its true motion, and the relative motion of the target.

After you have placed T00 at the location of the initial observation, you can construct the T—R line describing your ship's course and speed. You are on a course of north at 20 knots. R will be placed *ahead* of T one ring or 20 knots in distance, just as you did in relative motion except that here you are plotting forward from T to R instead of astern, from R to T. Operating on the six-mile range, Point R will be labeled R3. At the same time you mark T, it is helpful to place a dot over your ship's location as this will give you a better estimate of speeds of the various targets compared to your speed.

With Points T and R marked along with the dot indicating the time 00 position of your ship, you are free to settle back, turn off your plotting light, and watch the plot develop. You will see the target continuing to leave a west-to-east tail behind. Your ship as well will leave a tail behind if your display allows a dot of light to mark your position. At this point you will also notice that if you have your range rings turned on bright, they almost develop a life of their own as they move forward. To prevent them from putting great, smeary loops all over the screen, it is best to turn them to absolute minimum brightness.

After about two minutes of observation, you should be able to obtain a very close approximation of the target's course and speed by eye. The direction of true motion is obvious from the track of the target's tail. The speed of true motion may be estimated by comparing its length to the tail behind your ship or the distance between the dot you placed over your initial position and your present position. The ability to obtain a quick appreciation of relative speeds is very handy if you have to plan an escape maneuver.

At time 03, you see the situation as it appears in Figure 57 B. The Point M3 which marked the location of the target at time 03 lines up with R3. Whether you use true or relative motion, the message of this plot is the same: When R and M line up with your ship and the range is decreasing, you are in a collision situation.

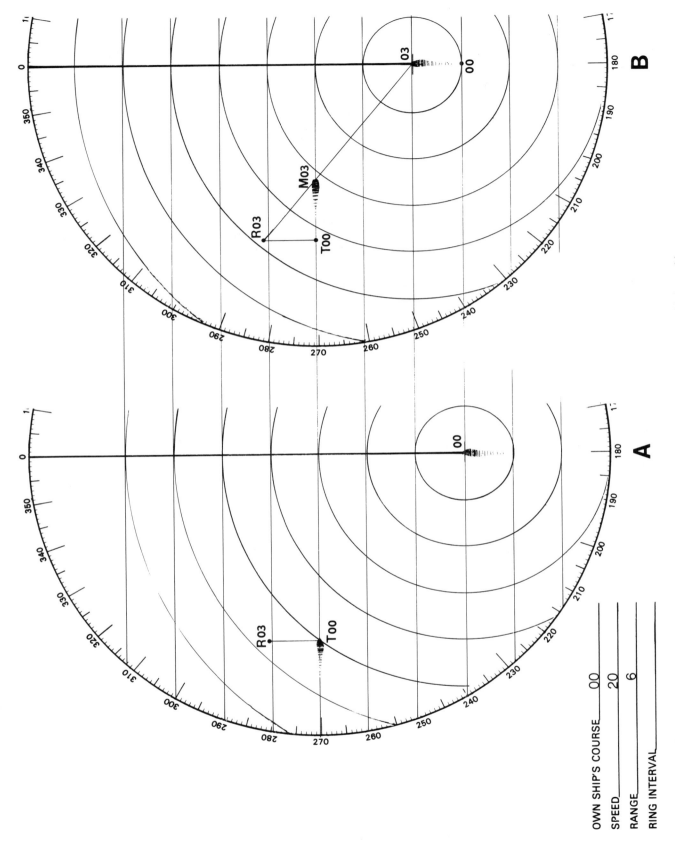

OWN SHIP'S COURSE   00

SPEED   20

RANGE   6

RING INTERVAL

Figure 57. A. Beginning the T—R—M plot. B. The T—R—M plot completed. Note motion of your own ship's position from 00 to 03.

59

A MANEUVER PLOTTED IN TRUE MOTION

Plotting a collision avoidance maneuver in true motion is essentially the same as in relative motion. Naturally, there has to be a difference, but it is a small one. When you plot an avoidance maneuver in true motion, it is best done on an instantaneous basis. This is the same type of process that you used when learning relative motion plotting, before you began to allow for decision and maneuvering time. Referring to Figure 58 A, you will see that the basic T—R—M plot is the same as in Figure 57 B. At time 03, on the clock and in the plot, a new relative motion or clearance line was added, passing one ring ahead. That's where you would like the target to go. This line is carried back into the plot just as before. The only difference is that, at this moment, no allowance will be made for plotting, thinking, and maneuvering time. That will come later. Now, pivot the T—R line on T as before, swinging R down to meet the new R—M line at Rc. Rotate the parallel grid cursor to line up with T—Rc and read your new course of 318°.

At this point, your experience tells you that a turn to 318° just won't work. It fails to allow for the normal, necessary delays that must occur before you can make your maneuver. The target has moved away from the departure point 03, and you haven't even begun to maneuver. To overcome this, it is necessary to add to your maneuver in order to make it come out right. In this case, depending upon your reaction time and your ship's ability to respond, you may want to add between 15° and 30° to your original estimate. Experience is the only thing that will help you to judge the amount necessary to add. That's not much help, but nobody ever said that true motion was the easiest method of collision avoidance plotting!

THE RETURN TO BASE COURSE

Assume that you have just completed the plot in Figure 58A which tells you that your calculated new course is 318°, you know you must add to the turn to make up for the various delays you'll encounter. Therefore, you decide to add 20° and have begun a left turn to 295°. Now, during the time that you are in the turn, you should consider whether it might be a good time to reset the true motion display so as to allow yourself the greatest possible view forward. Remember that your display center is always moving in the direction of your headflash, and you could lose a great deal of forward vision if you don't reset frequently. While you are in the turn and the plot is fresh in your mind, it is a good time to do this. Figure 58 B shows your turn completed, the scope center offset toward the lower right of the screen giving you maximum vision ahead and the target passing to the north.

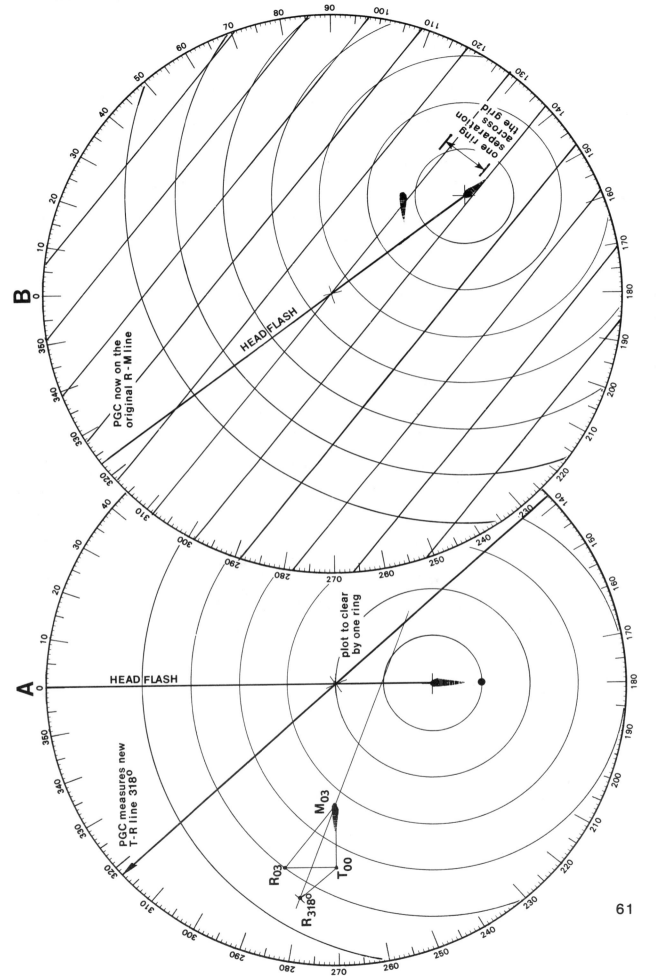

Figure 58. A. The collision avoidance plot in true motion. B. The use of the PGC to determine when to return to base course.

A

HEAD FLASH

PGC measures new
T-R line 318°

plot to clear
by one ring

M_{03}

R_{03}

T_{00}

$R_{318°}$

B

PGC now on the
original R-M line

HEAD FLASH

one ring
separation
across
the grid

61

In order to know when to return to your original course, use the parallel grid cursor set to the original R—M line; just as you did before when using relative motion. The difference lies in how you measure the actual clearance. In true motion, with the grid set to the original R—M, you measure the separation between your ship's position at any moment and the position of the target at the same moment. Note that the separation between ships is measured *across* the lines of the PGC, at right angles to them. In Figure 58 B there exists exactly one ring of separation between the target and your ship. If you were to return to your original course *now,* you would obtain exactly a one-ring CPA. Naturally, you can't make instantaneous returns to course any more than you could when taking your first avoidance action. Therefore, it is necessary to anticipate the moment of return and start back just before the target image reaches the desired separation. Again, it's a matter of skill and judgment in estimating the precise moment.

Here, briefly, is a review of the steps involved in plotting and executing a collision avoidance maneuver in true motion.

1. Construct the T—R—M plot.
2. Draw from M a clearance line past your ship's position at the desired CPA.
3. Bring this new DRM line into the plot, crossing the T—R line.
4. Begin maneuver immediately—traffic permitting.
5. Move R relative to T to indicate the necessary course or speed change.
6. Add to the indicated maneuver sufficient additional action to allow for your delay in completing the change.
7. Reset the scope as desired.
8. Observe the bearing of the target; it should now be changing.
9. Set the PGC to the original DRM.
10. Observe the separation of the target and your ship's position across the PGC.
11. Return to your base course when you are separated from the target by the desired CPA.

BASIC ELECTRONIC AIDS IN TRUE MOTION

Several manufacturers are now providing electronic devices which assist the radar operator in the estimation of risk of collision when in the true motion mode. The most basic and simplest of these is the EBL (electronic bearing line). Decca radars are equipped with this device under the trade name Interscan. Whichever you may encounter, its proper use will greatly simplify estimation of the risk of collision when using true motion.

Figure 59 A shows a true motion plot begun at time 00. The original position of your ship is shown by the time mark 00. A dot placed over the target at this time is properly marked T0 and the T—R line constructed to Point R3. Also, at time 00, the EBL (or Interscan, if you are using a Decca radar) is extended from your ship's position to the position of the target. This appears in the figure as a dashed line. The end of this line is Point T and is also marked R0M0. This is because the target (Point M) and the end of the EBL (Point R) will all depart from this point to develop the complete plot.

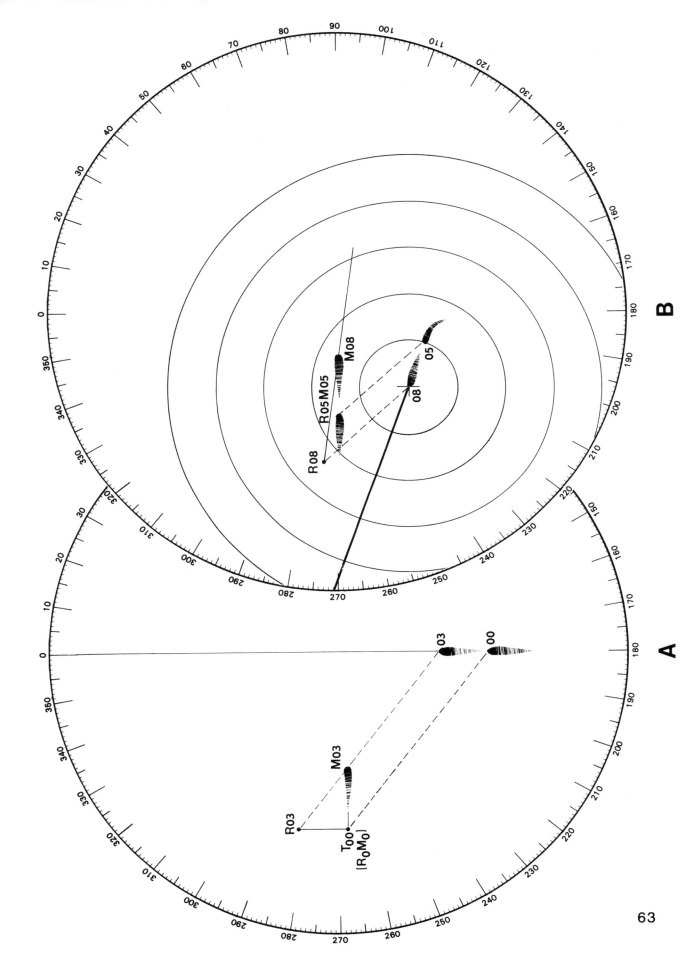

Figure 59. A. The use of the Interscan or EBL to determine risk of collision. B. At 05, the EBL is placed on the target. Three minutes later, the end of the EBL is well away from the target showing a large CPA.

63

Now, as the plot develops, several things may be seen to happen. First, of course, the target moves away from Point T along its true motion path. Your ship's indicator, the end of the EBL, also leaves Point T moving north in the direction of your headflash, along the T—R line. At minute 03, the end of the dashed EBL is at Point R03 while the target has moved to what will be marked as M03. Your ship has advanced from position 00 to 03. Now the use of the EBL will become apparent.

After you have set the EBL on a true motion target, *the end of the EBL will represent Point R while the target's position at the same instant will represent Point M.* If you now follow the progress of Points R and M as described above, from T0, you will see that, in this case, they always line up with your ship's position. This is most easily seen in the plot at time 03. Whenever R and M line up with your vessel and the range is decreasing, you know you have a collision predicted.

In practice, you may estimate the risk of collision quickly and easily by this method. Merely place the EBL on a target and wait until the end of the line (call it Point R) and the target (Point M) have separated sufficiently so that you can sight from R to M toward your ship's position at that moment. This line shows you the projected CPA and thus, the risk of collision.

Figure 59 B shows this method in use after a course change to avoid collision. At time 05 you have steadied up on a course of 290°. The target is at the point marked R05M05, and the EBL has been placed on the target. Now, as your vessel moves on its course of 290°, toward the point marked 08, the target moves along its true course toward the point marked M08. The end of the EBL will separate from the target, winding up eventually at R08. The relative motion of the target at any time may be estimated by sighting from the end of the EBL to the target's position at the same moment. This has been done for you at time 08 and is the line R08M08. You can see that this line now clears your ship's position by more than one ring indicating a safe passing distance.

This is certainly a difficult and time-consuming method of estimating the risk of collision. In any multiple target situation, you would probably be better off using relative motion.

10. Proper Radar Tuning

Before the radar can be used for plotting or collision avoidance, it must be able to present a reasonable picture of the surrounding area: landmasses, buoys, anchored vessels, and, of course, vessels under way which might threaten your vessel. Often, apparently minor deviations from ideal tuning are sufficient to cause loss of targets, especially those beyond "middle range" of about six miles. The biggest problem is that there is no way to indicate that the radar is not, in fact, properly tuned. The radar merely returns the message that "all's well" when, in fact, there might be a large number of targets out there waiting to surprise you. Proper tuning of the radar can eliminate most of these surprises.

The most natural first step in tuning the radar would seem to be to "turn it on." There are, however, several steps that must be performed, if not before the radar is turned on, then certainly before it warms up. If you are unfamiliar with a particular set, it is best to make these checks before the "power is on" stage. After becoming accustomed to the position of the various controls and the sequence of operation, you will find that there is sufficient time to accomplish all that's necessary between the moments when the power is on and the set is ready to operate.

The first two steps designed to protect the radar from damage are:

1. Turn the antenna *on*.
2. Turn the "brightness" or "intensity"
control *off*.

These steps will protect the CRT (cathode ray tube) from (a) being burned by the sweep stopped in one place for too long a time and (b) being damaged by the brightness control being set too high.

After having performed these steps (ignoring 1. if your set doesn't have a separate antenna switch), you may then do the following (while waiting for the CRT and other tubes to warm up—at least one minute on the average):

3. Turn the STC (sea clutter) to zero—*off*.
4. Turn the FTC (rain clutter) to zero—*off*.
5. Set the gyro repeater, if fitted, to the
same heading as the master gyro.

At this point, some radars will operate differently than others. Some will give you a rotating sweep or time base, although no targets will be visible, while others will show merely a blank screen. Those showing a blank screen require a waiting period usually of three minutes after the transmitter has been turned on. If you have a radar that shows a sweep after one minute or so, you may perform the following adjustments while waiting for the transmitter to come on line:

6. Set the master brightness or intensity
control so that a sweep becomes *barely*
visible. "Barely," in this context, means
that if you look twice at the display, the
sweep is so faint that one time you think
you see it and another time, you think you
don't!
7. Set the range ring intensity.
8. Set the headflash intensity—if
adjustable.

9. Check and adjust the centering of the presentation.

Note—Proper intensity of the rings and headflash demands that they be no brighter than the dimmest target.

If the radar blanks the screen while the transmitter is in its warm-up cycle, you must wait until full power is on before beginning step 6. Once you have completed steps 6 through 9, continue as follows:

10. Select either the three- or six-mile range, or whatever range your unit has close to these.
11. Turn the gain control toward its most sensitive position. If you obtain a picture before reaching the end of rotation you may stop at that point.
12. Adjust the tuning control for *maximum* target and noise display.
13. Reduce the gain setting until only a small amount of background speckle remains.
14. Repeat steps 12 and 13 to insure that the tuning is peaked and that no further improvement is possible.

At this point you should be able to see any targets and landmass areas within the three- to six-mile range you have selected. Your presentation is complete with range rings and headflash, and it should be easy to make a quick assessment of risk of collision, should there be any. If not, you may complete the tuning and set up procedure as follows:

15. Adjust the STC control to permit viewing any targets which might be obscured by sea clutter.
16. Adjust the FTC control to view any targets which might be obscured by rain.

Note—Proper use of these controls is to use the least amount of suppression and to check the settings often as conditions change.

Now, you have completed the basic tuning of your radar. It is a good idea to scan the various ranges to check for more distant land and targets. This will also serve to verify the proper tuning of your equipment. Selecting *long pulse* mode will enhance target acquisition and appearance at longer ranges.

Correct operation of your radar demands that you check the controls frequently to verify their proper setting. This is done by adjusting the gain, tuning, intensity, and clutter while watching the screen. In each case, you are trying to improve the quality of the radar picture which ideally should show large, bright targets against a black background with light speckle indicating noise and clutter.

IMAGE PERSISTENCE

Throughout this book the radar images shown in the illustrations have been given "tails" or persistence tracks. These tracks are the afterimage which remains when a target has moved to another location. The length of time that this afterglow remains visible is a factor of the relative darkness of the area surrounding the radar and the "persistence" value of the PPI (plan position indicator) scope itself.

The persistence value is expressed in two ways. A "short persistence" scope is one on which the afterimage disappears comparatively rapidly. This is often characteristic of unstabilized radar as well as older sets in which the cathode ray tube hasn't been replaced for a long time. Stabilized radar is usually provided with a "long persistence" tube which is designed to show the "tail" tracks clearly over a longer period of time.

Radar display tubes manufactured in the United States are also given a designator which expresses the persistence level. This designator is known as the P, or phosphor number. Phosphor is the chemical compound on the face of the tube that provides the actual glow. The higher the number, the longer will be the persistence. Most of the older unstabilized radar units had a tube designated P-9, although there were many designated as P-7 and P-11 as well. The more modern stabilized radar units use a longer persistence formulation in the neighborhood of P-22. If a replacement CRT that has the ability to display the target track as a persistence tail is needed, you should make sure you have a display tube installed that is of this type. Darkening the viewing area is also essential.

11. The U. S. Coast Guard Examinations

Many of you who read this book have already successfully passed one or more examinations on the use of radar and radar plotting. Despite this fact, one seldom approaches taking an examination with the idea that it will be easy. Many of you will be put off merely by the fact that someone in authority is about to challenge you to demonstrate how much you know. Often, that is all it takes to turn a competent deck officer into a bundle of nerves.

There is a way around the problem, however. To begin with, if you presently hold a U. S. Coast Guard license, very likely you have already passed one or more of these examinations. If you've done it before, you can do it again. On the other hand, if you haven't taken a Coast Guard exam, and the radar simulator is a total mystery, you may take consolation in the fact that many thousands of people have managed to survive these tests. The odds are very strong that you will survive as well, especially if you accept the suggestions given in this chapter. First of all, be totally aware of the type of exam you will take. Also, be sure you have access to the tools you will need to deal with the plotting situation.

The Coast Guard plans soon to abandon all paper plot examinations in favor of radar recertification or upgrading using a simulator. In a few remote locations where simulators are not available the paper plot examinations may still be employed. Both types of examination will be discussed here and even though you might as well plan on taking the simulator exam, it would be wise to familiarize yourself with the paper plot quiz too. Both will provide invaluable practice and familiarity with the basic plot, the "six solutions," and the mechanics of collision avoidance geometry.

THE PAPER PLOT EXAM

First, consider the paper plot examination. Just about everybody who has ever sat for a Coast Guard license has taken at least one of these. In this book, there are four sample "Coast Guard type" examinations (see Chapter 12) which will provide 40 questions to practice on. The questions and plots are taken from actual examinations that were in use and have been changed only in certain details so as not to compromise the "real" exams.

In the actual exam, you will be asked to answer twenty questions arranged in two groups of ten. Each of these groups must be passed with a score of at least ninety average. This means that you can miss only two answers altogether. Any more and you fail. You also have to accomplish this minor miracle in twenty minutes—*That's only two minutes per question!* Now that may seem like pretty tough odds, but there are several things you can do to even things out a bit.

First, you should become as familiar as possible with the basic plot, the six numerical solutions, and the process involved in making a collision avoidance maneuver. Notice from reading the practice questions that some are really easy—What is the DRM of Target A?—while others are real "bears"—What maneuver will best avoid collision or close quarter situations with all targets? Now, while you have the time, study these questions and their solutions carefully. If you do this, you won't have to waste time once you are taking the exam itself.

As a rule, you are allowed all the time you need to read the questions before the examination. (You are not given the plot sheet with the target locations marked on it, just the question sheet.) Read the questions carefully before indicating that you are ready to begin. If you have any queries about meaning or interpretation, ask them at once and not while the clock is running. Naturally, the examiner isn't going to review plotting techniques or indulge in lengthy "how-to" sessions, but he should, if approached reasonably, be able to define, for example, just what is meant by the term "close quarters" in question three or the abbreviation "TCPA" in number nine.

There may be a question about what tools you are allowed to bring into the paper plot exam. Basically, you should be able to answer all questions using only a pencil and straightedge. Most examination centers allow only the use of a pencil and two 45° triangles. However, it is possible that one or two examiners have permitted dividers as well. It is a good idea to check ahead with the office where you will sit for the exam. In that way, you can avoid the shock of learning at the last minute that the one method you have practiced isn't allowed.

To use the time allotted most efficiently, the first thing you should do is construct an R—T—M plot on all targets. One of the things that is going to make it possible for you to work one problem on an average of two minutes, is the fact that once you have the basic plot drawn on your paper, you can extract a lot of answers from it without further drawing or measurement. For example, refer to Figure 22. Two plots are shown. If you were asked the direction of true motion of Target A, and the choices were 000°, 045°, 090°, and 135°, you probably would have no trouble at all choosing 045° as the correct answer. Remember, all the paper plot exams are multiple-choice type (or *multiple-guess* as some call it) and you need only pick the *best* answer of the choices offered.

If you find that there is no answer given in the choices that exactly matches the solution you have calculated, choose the one that is closest. For example, you plot the DTM of Target A as being 50° but the nearest choices are 45° and 90°. In this case, pick the choice nearest to your value, 50°. Naturally, if you don't find any choice that is close to your calculated value, make a quick recheck of your method. You have probably made an error somewhere.

Well, that didn't take very long. Just for practice, look again at the plots of Targets A and B. It doesn't take much imagination or time to see that the CPA of A is about 1.5 miles or that the DRM of B is about 225°. Any choice close to these values should be the right one, and you need not waste time with additional measurement. The only time you might want to break that rule is when there are one or more answers close to the one you have chosen. Then, you are stuck with making a quick determination of the exact value.

Now, what about the tougher questions? The ones that may begin—"If you change course 60° to the right to 110°T at time 09, what will be the new CPA of Target C?" Well, even these may often be eyeballed depending upon the choices given. (Refer to Chapter 2 on the DRM rules, if necessary, before continuing.) For instance, imagine your ship turning 60° to the right in the plot of Target B in Figure 22. If you had two answers for the new CPA of zero and one mile, you'd know immediately that neither could be the correct one. Your CPA is already better than two miles, and a right turn can only open that distance further.

Well, if there are four answers, you've already eliminated half of them. Now, it's just a choice between the remaining pair. One of these is for a new CPA of three miles while the last answer is for four miles or more. Here, you might want to do a quick plot, but probably you can look at that and figure out that 60° is a pretty hefty turn, and in all probability, will give you much more than just a mile additional clearance. So, choose the "four miles or more" answer, and hustle along to the next problem.

What if you hit a problem that you just can't answer, or that you think would take too much time to answer? That's easy: just skip that one and head off to the next. Make a mark next to the problem number that will let you know that you skipped it. When you have finished all the easier problems, you can go back to the one or two you have marked for later attention. This way, you will be assured of having given the maximum amount of time and effort to the largest number of easily answered questions which will give you the best chance to score well.

Now you are down to the last minute or two. You have one problem yet to do and another left behind. With two blank answers, you bilge the exam for sure. Quickly take a look at the last problem. It might be an easy one, and so have a go at it. If not, then take an educated guess. Maybe you can eliminate one or two obviously incorrect answers and be left with the odds-even chance that your blind pick will be correct.

Likewise, with the tough one you passed by, at least mark one of the answers. Better a chance at hitting one out of four or five than the certainty of losing on one left blank. You already have learned radar plotting and collision avoidance, and so while you are before the examiner, you should take advantage of every legal opportunity you have to improve your score.

THE SIMULATOR EXAM

With the inauguration of the radar simulator examination replacing the paper plot, the Coast Guard has removed itself from the radar-examining business. The various examining points are now operated by schools and private agencies with Coast Guard approval and certification. Unless you are a member of a union which operates an approved facility or can make some special arrangements, you will have to pay to take the exam and any classroom work that precedes it.

Various refresher courses are available. For instance, at the Seattle location, you may take a course lasting eight days, a three-day refresher, or the one-day "quickie." Each of these ends with the simulator exam. The cost of all this isn't small, especially when you consider that you also have to pay for transportation to and from the school plus your living expenses while in attendance. Thus, it is in your best interest to make certain you take all but not more schooling than you really need. If you are about to choose one of these courses, the information in this book will give you an idea of your capabilities and help you pick the training that will be best for you.

It may surprise you to know there is no "standard" examination used in simulator testing as there was in the case of the paper plot. Each examining center has had its curriculum and examination reviewed by the Coast Guard and has been approved for original license, renewal, or upgrading. The exact details of the instruction and testing are left to the discretion of the facility with the proviso that they meet certain critical standards. Thus, among the various testing centers you will find small differences in the type of instruction and the examination. Whichever school you attend will brief you thoroughly, including an explanation of these differences, before you take your examination. Therefore, the following examination as outlined, while very useful for study, is offered only as a "typical" example.

Your examination begins with an operational radar. To function smoothly and accurately throughout the test make certain you understand the location of essential controls before beginning. Know where the range switch, plotting scope light, parallel grid cursor, and other essential items are. Be sure you have your plotting pencil and a speed/distance scale or its equivalent in hand and that the room lighting is correct for proper observation of the targets and plot. In other words make certain you are ready in all respects (a quick trip to the head is a good idea, too).

Your examination will probably be run mostly on the 12-mile range. At time zero, or when the problem first begins, you should look out one range farther to see if there are any targets which will be coming onto your scope several minutes after the beginning of the run. This will avoid your attention being concentrated on a nonthreatening target while a real threat is being overlooked. If a target is at the outer edge of the scope or arrives after the start of the run, don't plot it until it has come onto the scope in about one range ring distance. There are two reasons for this. First, if you plot a course change maneuver, you need to be able to extend the new R—M line back through the plot so as to have room to swing the T—R line. If your "R" point is right at the rim of the plotting scope, this becomes impossible. Secondly, on most radarscopes, measurements made at the outer edge tend to be less accurate than those made a few inches farther inward. Also, some manufacturers use a plotting scope that has a severe upward curve at the edge. These conditions compromise your accuracy. So remember, try to wait until the target is in about one ring before you start.

Before beginning you should review Chapter 3 on basic R—T—M plotting if you are unfamiliar with the techniques involved. Plot all targets. Even if it is a buoy off to port or a fast target ahead, you should always get at least an "R" and "M" point designated. Then, if necessary, you can always place "T" later and continue plotting normally. But be sure to get the "R" and "M" points marked.

You will be required to complete a plot on the most threatening target, the one that will pass closest to your ship at the earliest time. You will derive the 6-problem solutions for this vessel, DRM through STM, and write them on your scope. You will also maneuver to obtain a one-ring, two-mile CPA on the threatening target and return to your base course and speed. You must do all this within a certain time. A good estimate of time allowed might be 25 minutes from start for the completion of your 6 numerical solutions and 35 minutes to take avoidance action and return to base course and speed. Remember, these figures may vary from place to place but not by any great amount.

You are allowed whatever maneuver you choose. You may turn right, left, reduce speed, or perform a combination of these. You may not, however, attempt a great number of random actions even though they might manage to get the desired CPA. Basically, you are allowed three actions. If your first maneuver gives you the CPA you desire, that's beautiful. If it doesn't, then make a second maneuver to get the CPA you want. You are then allowed a third maneuver to return to your base course and speed. That is a total of two actions to get rid of the target and one to come back to base course and speed on. Any more maneuvering and you lose points. Thus, you want to be sure that your first action is sufficient and if for some reason it fails to give the desired CPA, it is essential to get everything you need and a bit more with the second. Then, all you have to do is wait for the proper moment to return to base course and speed.

You may be presented with several targets. There will, however, be only one target with less than a two-mile CPA. For this target only, you will be required to determine and submit to the examiner the following information:

> 1. Direction of relative motion.
> 2. CPA.
> 3 Speed of relative motion.
> 4. Time of CPA.
> 5. Direction of true motion.
> 6. Speed of true motion.

You will also be judged on the following points:

> **7. The quality of your plot.**
> **8. That you maneuver your vessel in accordance with the Rules of the Road and obtain a two-mile CPA on the original threatening target and at least a two-mile CPA on all other traffic.**
> **9. That you complete the answers in items 1 through 6 above in the 20-minute time allowed. (This may vary according to the problem being run, and the actual time will be announced before the exam begins.)**
> **10. That you complete all of the above and return to base course and speed by the time allowed. (Usually 35 minutes.)**

The tolerances used to evaluate your answers are quite liberal. Direction may be within $+/-10°$, speeds within $+/-3$ knots, and time within $+/-3$ minutes. CPA, both from the original plot and that obtained with the threatening target, must be within $+/-½$ mile.

How does the requirement (point 8 above) that you "maneuver by the Rules of the Road" affect your choice of action? You should consider that you are in severely limited visibility and operating basically under the provisions of Rule 19. In effect, you are encouraged to turn to the right in preference to a turn to the left; to avoid turning in front of any vessel abaft your beam; to make one substantial maneuver rather than a number of small ones; and, in general, to conduct yourself in a prudent but decisive manner.

Remember, however, that you are *not* prevented from making a left turn, from changing speed, or from making a combination speed and course change. As in real life, you should first consider those actions that are preferable under the rules as well as those which are simple in their concept and implementation. Then, if these will not serve, seek alternatives. As yet, there has not appeared a Coast Guard exam in which a right turn was impossible.

The question of "how substantial is an adequately substantial maneuver?" is best left to the courts of admiralty. In the case of your maneuver in the radar simulator, "substantial" should be taken to mean "as much as you need to avoid the target in question plus a little more to be sure with." Don't, however, take such an excess of "extra", that you find yourself needlessly in conflict with another target which never should have been even a remote threat.

12. Practice Plotting Tests

The following four practice exams are designed to allow you to test your ability in applying certain principles and techniques. Naturally, a "paper" test isn't a very good approximation of reality, but it will serve to give you some idea of your ability to handle plotting situations.

If you wish to attempt a "Coast Guard" type exam situation, have all your plotting materials handy plus a clock with which to time yourself. Read through the section on taking the paper plot exam and follow the suggestions given. Before beginning, read through all the questions first and make certain you understand any abbreviations used as well as the intent of the questions. Allow twenty minutes by the clock and then score yourself. (A grade of 90% or better was required for passing.) If you miss a question, be sure you read through the analysis, and review any part of the text that will serve to put you on the right track.

Remember it is ridiculously easy sometimes to misread a "DRM" instead of the desired "DTM," or to take a measurement to the fourth ring rather than the four-mile mark. So again: *Do read the questions carefully. Assume nothing that isn't stated. Good Luck!*

PLOTTING TEST 1

1. You expect to pick up a radar reflector equipped buoy on your watch. Which of the contacts, if any, would you evaluate as a buoy?

        A. A
        B. C
        C. D
        D. No contact is a buoy

2. Assume contact A maintains course and speed. When contact A has closed to 4 miles, to what course should you come, maintaining your speed of 20 knots, so that A will pass down your port side with a CPA of 2 miles?

        A. 010°
        B. 030°
        C. 053°
        D. 070°

3. Assume your vessel and all contacts maintain course and speed. Contact A will be 4 miles away at minute:

        A. 11
        B. 14
        C. 17
        D. 20

4. Assume your vessel and contact B maintain course and speed. When B is dead ahead, what navigational light(s) would you expect to see?

        A. Masthead, range, and green sidelight
        B. Masthead, range, and red sidelight
        C. Masthead, range, and red and green sidelights
        D. Stern light

5. The approximate true course and speed of contact B is:

        A. 260° at 12 knots
        B. 295° at 10 knots
        C. 320° at 30 knots
        D. 355° at 16 knots

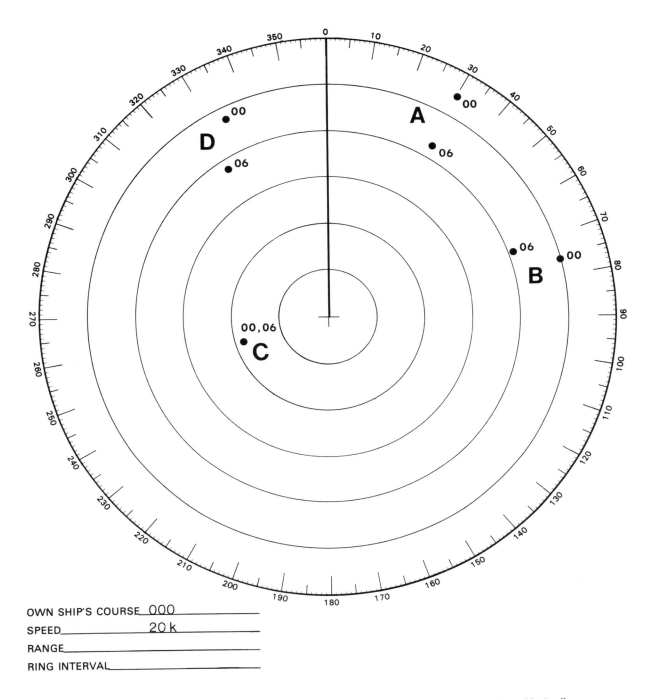

OWN SHIP'S COURSE 000

SPEED 20 k

RANGE

RING INTERVAL

Figure 60. Your own ship's course is 000° at 20 knots. The range is 12 miles and the ring interval is 2 miles.

6. The SRM of contact D is greater than that of contact C. However, the true speed of D:

  A. Is less than that of C
  B. Is greater than that of C
  C. Is the same as that of C
  D. Cannot be compared to that of C from the information available

73

7. Assume all contacts maintain course and speed. If you stop your vessel DIW (dead-in-the-water), contact C will:

    A. Maintain a steady bearing and range
    B. Develop a DRM of 000° and an SRM of 20 knots
    C. Develop a DRM of 180° and an SRM of 10 knots
    D. Maintain a steady bearing with decreasing range

8. Assume all contacts maintain course and speed. If you stop your vessel DIW, contact D will:

    A. Decrease its SRM
    B. Increase its SRM
    C. Maintain the same DRM and SRM
    D. Maintain the same SRM with an opposite DRM

9. Assume all contacts maintain course and speed. At minute 07 you alter course to 045°, maintaining the same speed. Contact B will:

    A. Develop a steady bearing with decreasing range
    B. Fall to the left or counterclockwise (below the original R—M line)
    C. Fall to the right or clockwise (above the original R—M line)
    D. Continue along the original R—M line but with a reduced SRM

10. Assume all contacts maintain course and speed. Which of the following actions by your vessel would result in an increased CPA on all contacts?

    A. A reduction in speed to 5 knots
    B. An increase in speed to 25 knots
    C. A change of course to 320°
    D. A change of course to 045°

PLOTTING TEST 2

1. When contact A closes to 4 miles, you change course so as to pass A 2 miles ahead. The course to change to is:

    A. 010°
    B. 033°
    C. 053°
    D. 065°

2. All vessels maintain their course and speed. At what time will contact A be at a range of 4 miles?

    A. 09
    B. 12
    C. 18
    D. 21

3. When contact D closes to 2 miles, what lights would you expect to see?

    A. Masthead, range, and both sidelights
    B. Masthead, range, and port sidelight
    C. Masthead, range, and starboard sidelight
    D. Stern light

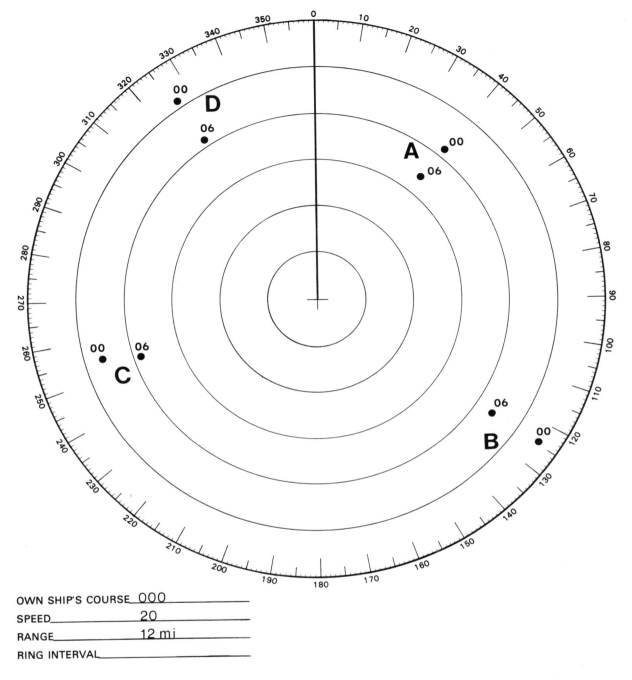

OWN SHIP'S COURSE 000

SPEED 20

RANGE 12 mi

RING INTERVAL

Figure 61. Your own ship's course is 000° at 20 knots. The range is 12 miles and the ring interval is 2 miles.

4. Contact C maintains course and speed. You increase your speed to 35 knots. How does this affect the SRM and DRM of contact C?

    A. The SRM increases, and the DRM passes ahead

    B. The SRM decreases, and the DRM passes astern

    C. The SRM increases, and the DRM passes astern

    D. The SRM decreases, and the DRM passes ahead

75

5. All contacts maintain their course and speed. If you maneuver at time 07, what is the best action for you to take to avoid a close quarters situation, less than 1 ring, on all targets?

    A. Slow to 15 knots
    B. Change course to 038°
    C. Maintain course and speed
    D. None of the above will result in a CPA of greater than 1 range ring

6. What is the true course and speed of contact D?

    A. 068° at 12 knots
    B. 103° at 18 knots
    C. 145° at 23 knots
    D. 046° at 20 knots

7. You may not alter course. When contact A reaches the 4-mile range, what speed change would you make to get a 2-mile CPA ahead?

    A. Stop—zero knots
    B. Increase speed to 25 knots
    C. Decrease speed to 12 knots
    D. Decrease speed to 7 knots

8. What is the true course and speed of contact A?

    A. 270° at 15 knots
    B. 210° at 10 knots
    C. 313° at 13 knots
    D. The contact is stopped (DIW)

9. If contact D stops DIW at minute 12, what will be his new DRM and SRM?

    A. 070° at 12 knots
    B. 095° at 16 knots
    C. 000° at 20 knots
    D. 180° at 20 knots

10. Your vessel maintains course and speed. The relative motion line of contact B begins to move above, to the right of, the original relative motion line. What has B done?

    A. Changed course to 270°
    B. Increased speed
    C. Increased speed and changed course to 270°
    D. Decreased speed

PLOTTING TEST 3

1. Assume your vessel and all contacts maintain course and speed. Contact A will be 4 miles away at minute:

    A. 07
    B. 10
    C. 13
    D. 16

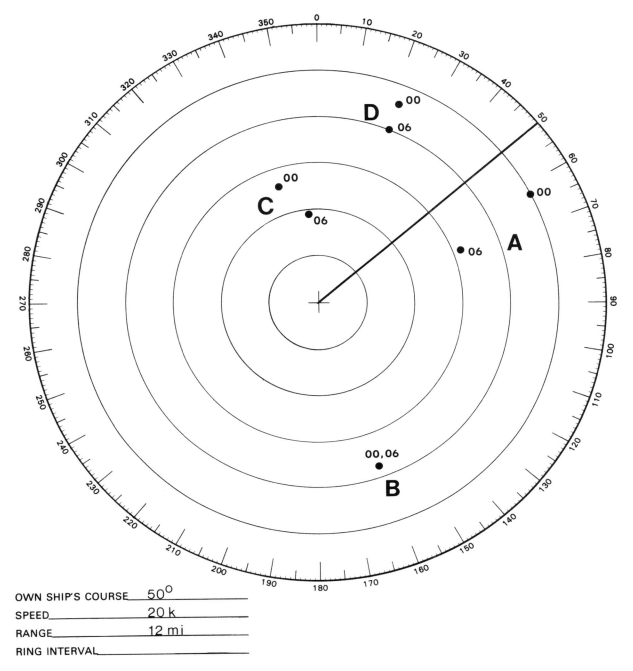

OWN SHIP'S COURSE ___50°___
SPEED ___20 k___
RANGE ___12 mi___
RING INTERVAL _____

Figure 62. Your own ship's course is 50° at 20 knots. The range is 12 miles and the ring interval is 2 miles.

2. The approximate true course and speed of contact C is:

        A. 268° at 25 knots
        B. 050° at 20 knots
        C. 087° at 28 knots
        D. 130° at 16 knots

3. Assume all contacts maintain course and speed. If you stop your vessel DIW, contact B will:

    A. Maintain a steady bearing and range
    B. Develop a DRM of 050° at 20 knots
    C. Develop a DRM of 230° at 10 knots
    D. Maintain a steady bearing with decreasing range

4. Assume all contacts maintain course and speed. At minute 10 you alter course 90° to the right maintaining the same speed. Contact A will:

    A. Develop a steady bearing with decreasing range
    B. Pass ahead with greater than a 2-mile CPA
    C. Pass ahead with less than a 2-mile CPA
    D. Continue along the same R—M line at an increased SRM

5. Assume all contacts maintain course and speed. Which of the following actions by your vessel at time 06 would result in an increased CPA on all contacts?

    A. A reduction in speed to 5 knots
    B. An increase in speed to 25 knots
    C. A change of course right to 070°
    D. A change of course left to 330°

6. You expect to pick up a radar reflector equipped buoy on your watch. Which of the contacts, if any, would you evaluate as a buoy?

    A. A
    B. B
    C. D
    D. No contact is a buoy

7. Assume your vessel and contact C maintain course and speed. When C is dead ahead, what navigational light(s) would you expect to see?

    A. Masthead, range, and green sidelight
    B. Masthead, range, and red sidelight
    C. Masthead, range, and both sidelights
    D. Stern light

8. The SRM of contact A is much greater than that of contact D. However, the true speed of A:

    A. Is less than that of D
    B. Is greater than that of D
    C. Is the same as that of D
    D. Cannot be compared to D from the information available

9. Assume contact A maintains course and speed. When A has closed to 4 miles, to what course should you come, maintaining your speed of 20 knots, so that A will pass down your port side with a CPA of 2 miles?

    A. 159°
    B. 090°
    C. 126°
    D. 183°

10. Assume all contacts maintain course and speed. If you stop your vessel DIW, contact B will:

    A. Decrease its SRM
    B. Increase its SRM
    C. Maintain the same DRM and SRM
    D. Maintain the same SRM with an opposite DRM

PLOTTING TEST 4

1. What is the approximate course and speed of contact D?

        A. 128° at 21 knots
        B. 308° at 22 knots
        C. 012° at 16 knots
        D. 192° at 16 knots

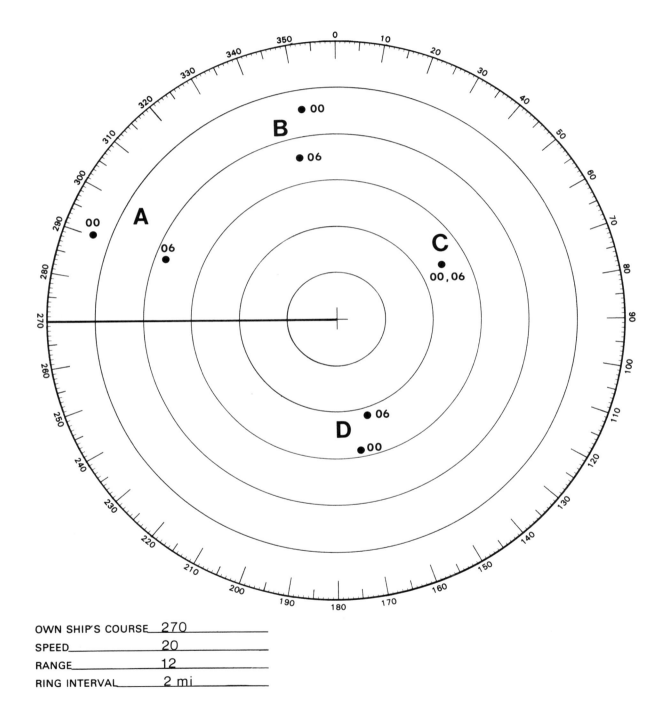

OWN SHIP'S COURSE __270__

SPEED _____ __20__

RANGE _____ __12__

RING INTERVAL _____ __2 mi__

Figure 63. Your own ship's course is 270° at 20 knots. The range is 12 miles and the ring interval is 2 miles.

2. Assume all contacts maintain course and speed. When contact A is at 4 miles, what course change would you make, maintaining your speed of 20 knots, to have A pass down your port side with a CPA of 2 miles?

      A. Left to 240°
      B. Left to 210°
      C. Right to 247°
      D. Right to 323°

3. The approximate time at which contact D will be at 4 miles range will be minute:

      A. 07
      B. 10
      C. 15
      D. D is past CPA

4. All contacts maintain course and speed. At minute 12, you alter course right to 315°. Contact C will pass you:

      A. Close aboard or collide
      B. Astern with a CPA of over 2 miles
      C. Astern with a CPA between 1 and 2 miles
      D. Ahead with a CPA greater than 1 mile

5. All contacts maintain course and speed. Which of the following actions taken at minute 12 would best avoid contacts A and D by at least 1 ring?

      A. Change course to 150°
      B. Change course to 305°
      C. Change course to 330°
      D. None of the above

6. All contacts maintain course and speed. At minute 12, you change speed to 10 knots. You then note that target C has begun to plot to the left (CCW) of his new R—M line threatening you with a close quarters situation. This would indicate that he probably:

      A. Changed course to the right
      B. Increased speed
      C. Changed course to the left
      D. Decreased speed

7. Your vessel and all contacts maintain speed until minute 12. At that time you sight the running lights of contact B. You would expect to see:

      A. Masthead, range, and green sidelight
      B. Masthead, range, and red sidelight
      C. Masthead, range, and both sidelights
      D. A white stern light

8. The true speed of contact B is:

      A. Less than that of contact A
      B. Greater than that of contact A
      C. The same as that of contact A
      D. Impossible to determine from the information available

9. If you stop your vessel DIW, contact C will:

        A. Close range with your ship
        B. Open range with your ship
        C. Pass under your stern
        D. Assume a steady range and bearing

10. Which contact presents the most immediate danger to your vessel?

        A. A
        B. B
        C. C
        D. D

ANSWERS TO PLOTTING TEST 1

1. C. Look for a contact moving parallel to your headflash opposite to your motion at an SRM of 20 knots. Be careful not to mix up the target designation letter with the letter indicating your choice of answer.

2. C. Extend the R—M line to the 4-mile (second) ring. Draw a clearance line from that point across your bow tangent to the 2-mile ring. Put this line into the plot through M. Pivot on T, swinging R to meet the new R—M line at Point Rc. The line T—Rc is your course to steer.

3. C. Step off the 6-minute R—M interval. Minute 18 occurs just inside the 4-mile ring. Call it 17 minutes to the 4-mile mark.

4. D. The vessel's heading as it passes ahead of you is 320°. You see only the stern light. Draw the outline of the vessel heading 320° as it crosses your headflash.

5. C. If you constructed your R—T—M plots before beginning the questions, you can just about eyeball this one. The only 30-knot speed is choice C, and this is the only choice where the T—M is faster than your ship.

6. A. Again, a quick look at the T—M vectors gives you the answer. Note that the entire first sentence is not relevant to the question and serves only as a "confuser."

7. B. When you stop your ship, all R—M becomes the same as the T—M.

8. A. As in question 7. Since the T—M is zero, when your ship stops, the R—M also becomes zero.

9. C. Plotting a 45° change on B, the new Rc—M line is upscope or above the original R—M line.

10. D. Slowing brings C upscope and closer. Increasing speed brings B downscope and closer. Changing left gets you into trouble with both C and D. The only remaining answer is the right turn to 045°.

ANSWERS TO PLOTTING EXERCISE, FIGURE 22

	Target A	Target B
DRM	77°	222°
CPA	1.4 miles	2.1 miles
SRM	33 knots	30 knots
TCPA	7.5 minutes	10.5 minutes
DTM	49°	264°
STM	40 knots	20 knots

ANSWERS TO PLOTTING TEST 2

1. B. After constructing all R—T—M plots, bring A's R—M line to the 4-mile (second) ring. Draw a clearance line one ring ahead. This is your new R—M line. Place this into the plot through M. Swing R around T to cross the new R—M line at Rc. T—Rc now indicates your course to steer.

2. C. A simple application of the basic R—T—M plot. Three "steps" of your divider set to the SRM put you right on the second ring. At 6 minutes per step, TCPA equals 18.

3. C. Step D down to the 2-mile ring. Remember that D is *heading* about 067°. Drawing a small ship outline on the R—M line will help you visualize the aspect of the vessel.

4. C. The DRM rules tell you that a vessel passing astern will pass farther astern when you increase speed. A quick plot shows that the SRM increases.

5. D. Try using the DRM rules first. Plot afterward to confirm your answer. Slowing brings C closer; changing to 030° just brings B in faster, and if you do nothing, A, B, and D all get you!

6. A. The T—M line tells you the answer.

7. C. Your plot from question 1 contains the answer. Where the new R—M line (Rc—M) crosses the original T—R line is the measure of speed.

8. C. Again, your original R—T—M plot has all the information you need. Just read it off between T and M.

9. D. Don't be confused by the "time 12" statement. *Whenever* another vessel stops, its DRM becomes the opposite of your heading (180°), and the SRM becomes whatever your ship's speed is (20 knots).

10. B. Contact B is faster than you. A change to 270° at any speed puts him astern, the DRM changing CCW. If he slows, he falls astern, again changing CCW. To change CW, to the right, he must increase speed.

1. B. After completing the plot on all targets, step off the R—M distance. The second (4-mile) ring falls between the 06- and 12-minute steps.

2. C. Measure the direction and length of the T—M line.

3. B. B is on the same course and speed as your vessel. If you stop, B will move at his true course and speed of 050° at 20 knots.

4. C. There are several points to note here. Your change is "90° to the right . . ." *of your present course*, or to 140° true. Don't make the mistake of turning to 090° true. Plot the new DRM: R140° to M and parallel this line down to the 10-minute position on the original DRM line. If you forgot to do this and picked answer B, be sure to go back and review the delayed action plot.

5. D. Look at the choices and try eyeballing this first. Note that the question refers to increasing CPA on *all* contacts. Any speed reduction brings B upscope reducing CPA. Increasing to 25 knots brings C closer. A 20° change right to 070° true gets you in trouble with both A and B. Left to 330° gets you away from A and B. C goes well upscope and D converts from collision to passing clear. Plot this maneuver against each target if you can't immediately grasp the logic of the DRM rules.

6. D. All targets show a definite STM so there can be no buoy on your scope.

7. D. When C crosses your headflash (dead ahead) his heading is about 086°. You are looking at his starboard quarter. If his heading were 140°, he would be heading at a right angle to you. At a heading of 118° or so, his sidelight, mast, and range lights should just disappear. When he is dead ahead, you will see only the sternlight.

8. B. The T—M of A is greater than the T—M of D. If you plotted all the targets at the start of the quiz, you could answer this one with no more than a *careful* glance. The use of the word "however" is a deliberate "confuser," designed to throw you off the correct answer. Learn to read a question for its essentials and ignore such underhanded tricks.

9. A. From the second (4-mile) ring, draw a clearance line passing the 2-mile ring on your port side. Bring this new R—M line into the plot through M. Swing R around T to intersect the new R—M line at Point Rc. Read your new course to steer from T to Rc.

10. B. B has no SRM initially. When you stop, if will develop an SRM of 20 knots.

ANSWERS TO PLOTTING TEST 4

1. B. You could eyeball this one if you completed the plot on all targets before starting. The T—M line shows the answer to be B.

2. D. Extend the R—M line to the 4-mile ring. Draw a clearance line from that point one ring ahead of your vessel. Put that line into the plot through M. Pivot R around T to meet the new R—M line at Point Rc. Read T—Rc to obtain your course to steer. Note that the T—Rc line falls just about on top of the Rc—M line. This is merely coincidence and has no significance.

3. A. D is almost at 4 miles at time 06. Another minute should do it.

4. B. T—R originally points to 270°. Construct a 20-knot T—Rc line pointing 315°. Now connect Rc to M, and you see that target C will pass 1½ rings astern.

5. C. Plotting the choices in order you will find: a change to 150° at time 12 puts you into close quarters with D. Right to 305° brings both targets inside the 2-mile ring. Changing to 330° gets rid of them both. Note that the question is similar in solution to number 2. Often you can find an answer to a question in the plot of an earlier problem.

6. C. This is an eyeballing type of question although, of course, you may also plot the answer. If you reduce speed, C, which was on the same course and speed with you, will begin overtaking you. Now, if C begins to move his DRM left, he must have changed course to the left.

7. B. DR target B ahead to time 12. The T—M line shows his heading to be about 228°. You would see all three lights.

8. B. A very easy ten points! B's speed is almost twice that of A.

9. A. C will immediately begin overtaking as the R—M becomes the same as the T—M.

10. A. A is the only target threatening a close quarters situation.

13. Automatic Radar Plotting Aids

You already know that collision avoidance is based on two requirements: one is the detection of a threatening target; and the other is the maneuver for avoidance of this target. It is also true that the size of the collision avoidance problem increases proportionally with the size of the vessels involved. Seen another way, the need for timely and accurate prediction is based on your vessel's ability to maneuver against the other vessel involved in the encounter. As an experienced ship's officer, you will agree anything that helps assure a competent level of prediction is of inestimable value. It just makes good sense to avail yourself of this type of information, especially if it is easily obtained, accurate, and intelligently presented. It has been the goal of the designers of ARPA (automatic radar plotting aids) equipment and those involved in drafting the regulations to assure that this easily understood level of information be displayed. How successful they have been in achieving this goal can only be judged by you, the user. It is the purpose of this section of *The Radar Book* to explain the operation of typical ARPA, in order to provide comparison of equipments, and to highlight particular features that can contribute to the easy understanding and use of the overall system.

THE REGULATIONS

Regulations, including Code of Federal Regulations (33 CFR 164.38) under the U. S. Port and Tanker Safety Act, called PTSA henceforth, of 1978 and Public Law Number 95474, plus pending changes to the SOLAS (Safety of Life at Sea) Convention, require that CAS (collision avoidance systems), ARPA, or ERMA (electronic relative motion analyzers) be fitted to all vessels exceeding 10,000 gross tons. Specifically, the PTSA requires that this be done by July 1, 1982, on any tank vessel or any vessel carrying hazardous cargo; that these vessels be equipped with an electronic relative motion analyzer which is at least functionally equivalent to such equipment complying with the specifications established by the U. S. Maritime Administration in August 1980. The U. S. government adopted the IMO (International Maritime Organization) recommendations as meeting the requirement of the PTSA. The IMO fitting schedule is recommended to begin on January 1, 1984, for all vessels over 40,000 gross tons and will require compliance—that is, complete compliance for all vessels over 10,000 gross tons by 1989.

THE NEEDS OF A COMPLETE SYSTEM

For those who are concerned that radar without additional enhancements will not be able to provide sufficient protection for the modern ship, reassurance is found in new high technology as the answer to reducing the collision threat. With ARPA, the ship's officer has even further help in managing his vessel. Yet, a wee, small voice keeps reiterating that ARPA, while enjoying the advantage of being automatic is, in fact, vulnerable to misuse and is dependent on the ability and understanding of the operator to produce the magic for which it was designed.

Unfortunately, overconfidence in the machine alone, is further encouraged by the extravagant claims of some manufacturers of this equipment. One of these claims is that "anyone can learn to use the device in five minutes." It is difficult to accept this claim when you consider evaluating a potential collision and applying the guidance given by the various readouts and displays of the device. Throughout this book, and particularly in this section, it is the intention of the authors to establish the interrelationship between equipment and operator firmly in the mind of the reader. While the interworkings of these electronics systems are of themselves a fascinating study, they will not be taken up in any great detail here. What is important is to correlate these automatic systems with the simple straightforward rules for handling collision threat and avoidance covered in earlier chapters. The number of collisions that occur during clear visibility (from five to ten nautical miles) continues to be a problem. The cause of collision frequently is a result of improper meeting, crossing, or overtaking maneuvers which can be attributed to a lack of understanding of the rules. Failure to reach an agreement with the opposing traffic concerning the

86

encounter, unsafe maneuvering based on the ambiguity or lack of whistle signals, lack of VHF communications in the initiation of dangerous maneuvers, and unexpected responses by the opposing traffic; all of these factors continue to plague the officer of the watch. An ARPA cannot entirely cure these ills, but it should contribute much to the understanding of the situation. It becomes obvious that, in addition to adequate equipment, the essential ingredients for a *complete* ARPA system are you and your good seamanship.

THE EQUIPMENT

A typical ARPA (automatic radar plotting aid) could be described as a computer-controlled or computer-enhanced device which displays visually the relative motion or true motion of a detected vessel or vessels which might constitute a collision threat. It, of course, requires input from a gyrocompass or any other method of getting a directionally stabilized reference. This reference can be a short-term input whose steady state needs only to be held from the initial observation throughout the maneuver. An input from your ship's own speed log is required to operate in true motion. The device, when used in the relative motion mode, can determine the relative speed by timing the movement of the contact between each sweep; and by this, arrive at the closing speed of the contact. In conjunction with the CRT display, readouts give additional pertinent information concerning the contact. The ARPA also provides a method with which the watch officer can determine the most likely means of avoiding a collision with this contact.

While the above will give you the essentials of a simple system, it is well to remember that the purpose of an ARPA is to reduce your work load as a radar observer by enabling you to handle more information on multiple targets and to provide continuous, rapid, accurate situation evaluations.

The functions of an ARPA include: detection, acquisition, automatic tracking, and display of up to 20 targets. In addition, visual or audio warnings for targets closing within a specified range are provided. Data displays present target bearing, target range, CPA, calculated target true course, and calculated target true speed.

A trial maneuver capability demonstrates the effect of a maneuver of your ship on all the contacts being tracked. This information is available without interrupting the present target data update and assists you in the decision-making process. As you consider all of its capabilities, the use of an ARPA begins to make sense.

ARPA INFORMATION AND ITS USE

Initially, information available from your ship's radar or from an ARPA take the form of a target display showing range and bearing on the scope. It is at this point that the ARPA starts to function as an automatic system by beginning the data processing that includes acquisition, target enhancement, and whatever noise rejection that may be required. If you have failed to observe the appearance of the target on your scope, nothing will happen until this target violates the guard ring zone you have previously set. Visual and/or audible warnings are provided to alert you, the watch stander, of any target which has violated the zone set. This warning requires you to consider action to reduce the threat implied by this signal. It is also at this point that you may decide to request additional information concerning the target. Present range and bearing, time, and distance of closest point of approach for this and other targets should, through target acquisition, be immediately available for this evaluation.

TARGET ACQUISITION

The feature of target acquisition, either automatically or manually, is an essential ingredient with all ARPA. From a persistent echo, the device gives you a target's range and bearing. For an automatic acquisition, the device usually requires a solid return for at least three sweeps before the built-in processor begins its function. This time interval varies with manufacturers, however, and once the data has been accepted by the processor, a smoothing occurs to maintain a good presentation even if an echo is lost for a sweep or two. The system is then "locked up" and will continue to display current data. If the echo disappears for a greater number of sweeps than is allowed for by the design model, the target drops out and must be reacquired. When it returns, the acquisition process starts all over again. Remember these actions are typical and you should, if possible, acquaint yourself with the features of the particular system aboard your ship.

A section of your ARPA known as *trial maneuver* permits you, the master or watch officer, to test the avoidance action you propose to take prior to initiating the actual maneuver. This facility will show the results you can expect by considering all the targets that are presently displayed on the scope. In other words, it is possible immediately to see the effect of a course or speed change on all tracked targets with reference to your ship. This provides the opportunity to assess the results of this change prior to making it, thereby assuring an adequate passing distance.

In some cases, you, the operator, can program the automatic mode to suppress acquisition of targets in areas where this information is of no interest. For example, you may, at this instant, not be interested in what is happening astern of your ship.

In its penultimate configuration, the ARPA will track and display information on at least twenty targets, manually or automatically acquired, and will indicate on the display which targets are being tracked. However, if a target passes near to another so that they appear to merge on the radar, the ARPA might swap one for the other. As far as you are concerned, this means the system begins tracking the wrong target. Most systems are designed to minimize this occurrence. However, be advised that this possibility exists regardless of how remote.

Whether your ARPA is interconnected with the ship's radar or is freestanding, it should, as a minimum, display all the information that would be typically available on the standard radar. Presentation of this information varies among manufacturers, but the device should at least be capable of presenting the situation in compass-stabilized relative or true motion, north up, or course up.

The situation can be displayed by a vector or, in some cases, by a graphic form where additional details are displayed in alpha-numerics using an additional CRT for this purpose. However, any information that deals with the prediction of target position must be available within a maximum of three minutes. This, of course, does not mean that the system is not useful during this time. Target's motion, as displayed on the CRT, establishes a trend. This motion trend includes the all-important relative motion of the target with reference to your ship.

A REVIEW OF KEY POINTS

On the outside chance that you might have missed something in reading the earlier portion of this section, a review follows. Even if it is information that you feel you have already grasped, you will be ahead by going over this material once more. Remember, what is being described is the typical ARPA and its use in a specific mode.

Display Mode

The display mode allows you to select either true motion, relative motion, north up, heads up, or course up. As you know, from your reading of earlier chapters of this book, each of these display modes has its particular advantages and disadvantages. Your judgment and good seamanship will determine which to use and when.

Target Acquisition

The system you are using must be capable of acquiring targets in both automatic and manual modes. As you should already understand, the device is compass-stabilized so that actions of your ship, yaw, and sudden course change can be compensated for. What you will see at any instant is the situation that is developing before any alarms demand your attention.

Automatic Acquisition

In automatic mode, your ARPA will, up to the limit of the system, mark threatening targets and usually designate by a priority symbol which targets need to be handled first. Your equipment should be capable of handling, as a minimum, up to 20 targets automatically in this mode. It should also be capable of suppressing acquisition in areas you might select. These areas would then be indicated on the display.

Manual Acquisition

As the name implies, in this case, you manually acquire a specific target by positioning the variable range marker and electronic-bearing line over it or a symbol designated to identify a target. This is done with either a joystick or a "track ball" to position the marker before pressing the target-acquiring button. Unlike the automatic mode a minimum of 10 targets is specified to be acquired manually. However, this varies with manufacturers and some are capable of up to 200.

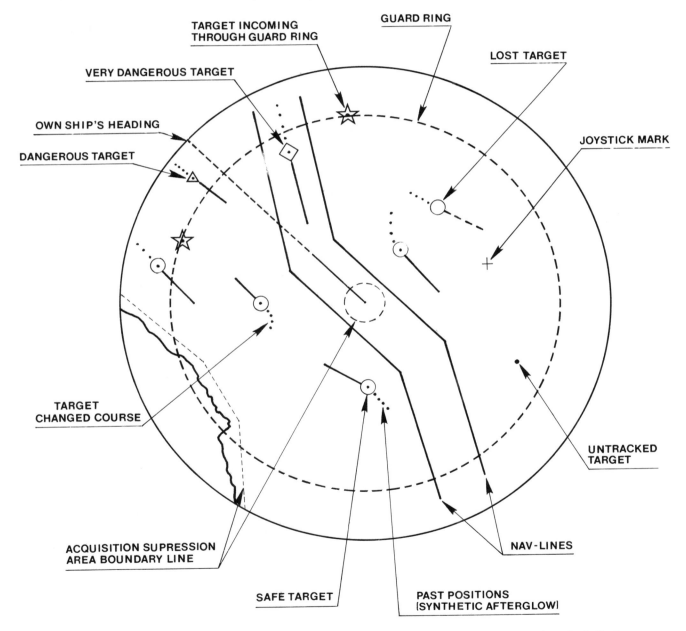

Figure 64. Typical ARPA north up stabilized display showing both vectors and afterglow whose lengths indicate your own ship or target speed.

Acquisition Suppression

As indicated above, you, the operator, can suppress contacts outside boundary lines that you, yourself, have set. If the situation involves a landmass, which you are not interested in, the boundary line can be drawn to exclude it and any other contacts. Each ARPA has its own peculiarities in the setting of these areas to be suppressed, so it would be best for you to review carefully the manual on your device.

Data Display Presentation

You will probably find that three different types of equipment are in use today. One type of ARPA is designed as a sideboy to function with your main radar. While the vector and alpha-numeric information it generates is displayed on the CRT of your main radar, all of the other information and controls required for its operation are located on the ARPA device. Another is the separate ARPA computer which is added to the existing radar display, and whose vectors will appear on your radar screen. The third consists of an ARPA unit which is entirely freestanding. This is preferred as it gives you the benefit of redundancy by essentially providing another radar on board, literally a "third display unit." It should be noted here, that two distinctly different approaches are taken in presenting collision avoidance information. One, the "pad" system, is a unique display in which an outlined area surrounds the target or a group of targets. The Sperry Company, who initiated this system, have provided instruction for its use in their advertising slogan Keep Off Our Pads. This literally describes how to interpret the display and how to maneuver your vessel using its information. The other approach uses "vectors" or "afterglow" (see Figure 64) to indicate the direction and speed of the true or relative motion of your ship and targets. To simplify the matter, the only form of presentation considered in this chapter on ARPA will be vectors.

Your ARPA should display at least the following range scales: 3, 6, and 12 miles. Most offer tracking facility for at least 24 miles; some have a tracking range of 48, 72, and up to 96 miles. The vectors display should be either time adjustable or have a fixed time scale. An alpha-numeric display of the time scale in use should be visible. For information that is displayed off "the scope," LEDs (light-emitting diodes) are most commonly used to alert you as to the data and the operating functions employed.

Numerical Displays

Numerical displays mounted on the panel or appearing on the CRT will provide specific target information such as bearing, course, CPA, distance, time to CPA, and speed. These displays also provide data about your ship's course and speed.

Alarm Presentation

It is essential that the data on which you are making your decision is good. In other words, it must be supplied by a properly operated, effective system; therefore, alarms are provided on the ARPA to advise you of a system failure. Included with the presentation is a lost target alarm, guard ring alarm, dangerous target alarm, and an alarm which denotes that the system is being saturated with over 20 targets. These alarms take various forms of flashing lights, buzzing, pinging, and other sounds.

Trial Maneuver Feature

This device simulates the course and speed of your ship and allows you to vary them with reference to an immediate target that is being displayed on the ARPA. By this technique you can determine the best course of action to take against this potentially dangerous threat. ARPAs can provide both a dynamic and a static trial maneuver with vectors to display graphically the results of an intended evasive maneuver. If the static trial is selected, your ship's vector changes to the chosen heading and reflects the speed entered manually. The new CPA resulting from the course change is usually read on a digital display and is also shown graphically. If this resulting CPA is unsatisfactory, your ship's course and speed may be changed until a desired, safe CPA is found.

Selecting a dynamic trial maneuver permits you, the operator, to see your ship move in true motion. For example, your ship moves across the PPI scope in the direction of the headflash, from the PPI center, showing its new position in relation to surrounding targets. In most cases the ARPA has the ability to include your ship's turning and stopping characteristics in the maneuver. With most of the present day equipment the action can be displayed at 30 times real time, i.e., each one-second movement equals one-half-minute. Thus you are able to see the results of a trial very quickly.

Special Features
Your ARPA will probably include such added features as:
- Navigation Line Display for fairway presentation. With this feature the channel which you plan to transit can be outlined by a series of lines giving you an immediate indication of the navigation constraints imposed by water depth, etc.
- Area Suppression. This keeps your ARPA system from acquiring targets in areas where no threat could exist, thus reducing the clutter of displayed information.
- Anchor Watch Alert. This allows a reference to be established that alerts the watch officer in the event the return signal moves beyond a specified area indicating anchor dragging.
- A Videotape Presentation. This provides a video recording of a specific area of interest which can be replayed on the CRT display.

GLOSSARY OF TERMS

Because of the competition among companies , the manufacturers of ARPA seldom interchange information in designing equipment to satisfy the regulations.

PTSA regulations that were drafted for ARPA did not deal with the problem of standardization of equipment, readouts, knobs, switches, and their placement; therefore, the regulations regarding ARPA do not specify these details. As a consequence, the arrangement of controls, the labeling of these controls, and the maximum capability of the equipment of various manufacturers vary considerably.

It is not likely that you will bother to learn all of the nomenclature of various manufacturers, but by giving you enough examples, this glossary should help you to feel comfortable with any brand name equipment you might encounter, making the transition from one to another easier.

The listing of the controls is arranged along the lines of a step-by-step description of the operation of the typical ARPA. The initial step, switching on your ARPA, should be completed before you get underway. It is usually a simple switch function that is accomplished by a rotary, push button, or rocker action. If your system is a freestanding display, in other words, a complete radar system, this is probably all you need to do for this step. If your ARPA is a sideboy that requires a companion radar perhaps two switch actions will be required. Starting with the power switch, this glossary gives several typical names of controls common to any ARPA.

1. Main Power, Mains, Power On-Off
This switch provides the overall on-off function. (Your main radar should be turned on also.)

2. Heading Set, Gyro Set, Gyrostat
On some ARPA, a flashing indicator reminds the officer to set the internal gyro after power is first turned on. This orients the PPI display so that the headflash indicates your ship's compass heading.

3. Radar Select, Video Source, Radar Control
On dual radar installations, this switch is used for choosing the radar to be used with ARPA. The selected radar must be properly tuned with the gain and anticlutter set to obtain the best results. Some ARPA provide internal automatic gain and anticlutter adjustments. Unless you are attempting to use the ARPA on its shortest range settings, make sure that the radar is set on long pulse. This will automatically set a low pulse repetition frequency thereby improving plotting capability. (See No. 8, Power Boost.)

4. Video Control, Radar Signal Modes, Video Select
This switch permits either normal video or quantized video to be shown on the ARPA. In the quantized

position partially processed radar video is displayed primarily for proper adjustment of anticlutter controls. In some cases the video control allows manual adjustment of gain, sea and rain return, or selection of automatic anticlutter.

5. Anticlutter Rain, Etc., Control
This switch reduces unwanted echoes such as areas of heavy precipitation or landmasses.

6. Anticlutter Sea, Etc., Control
This switch suppresses CRT display of reflections from nearby wave tops and heavy spray. The amount of sea clutter or sea return on a radar PPI will vary greatly with sea state and your desire (as the radar operator) to maintain contact and track small targets close to your ship. Proper adjustment of the STC and gain controls on the radar can eliminate most clutter without seriously reducing the signal from small targets of interest. Maximum application of STC will usually eliminate both small targets and sea clutter. This is obviously undesirable. As a result, most surface radars are operated with some sea clutter displayed on the PPI. Radar STC and gain controls should be adjusted to eliminate clutter signal saturation while still allowing target tracking in heavy clutter.

7. Range Selector, PPI Control
An appropriate range scale can be selected by this switch, i.e., .75, 1.5, 3, 6, 12, or 24 nautical miles. In some cases this is accomplished by push button with − (decrease) or + (increase) dependent on PPI display. In case of an add-on ARPA, the range scale selected need not be the same as the one in use on the radar. In fact, it may be important in some circumstances for the radar to be set at a greater range. The choice of range scale depends upon the circumstances, e.g., traffic density, rates of closing. Too short a range may result in being surprised by a fast target coming from ahead; too long a range in heavy traffic may result in confusion from the many vectors. Since the range may be instantly changed at will, you may use a short range to examine a close situation, execute trial maneuvers, and observe the maneuver. Then you can return the display to a normal, longer monitoring range. In certain manufacturers' radars, an extremely short pulse length and high PRF (pulse repetition frequency) are used with short radar range scales (1½ miles or less). This tends to reduce ARPA effectiveness.

8. Power Boost, Pulse Length Change
This control, when operated, will change the system's operation from short to medium pulse length on short ranges thereby enhancing the display of small objects nearby.

9. Brilliance Control, Brightness, Display Illumination
This continuously variable control permits adjustment of display intensity. The adjustment usually affects the brilliance of the radar video as well as the displayed target and your ship vectors.

10. Video Gain Control, Contrast, Gain
The control varies the strength of incoming video and noise. As a rule the correct setting is such that a speckled background is just visible on the PPI. If the gain is reduced to completely eliminate the speckled background, the result can be a reduction in target detection.

11. Range Ring Intensity, Range Ring Brilliance
This control regulates the display intensity of range marker rings.

12. Heading Marker, Flash Off, Suppress Head Marker
This spring-loaded on-off switch allows removal of the heading marker from the radar video display for one or more radar sweeps. Since a very weak echo could be masked by the heading marker line, you should use this switch to eliminate the possibility of missing a small echo that is directly ahead or coincident with the line.

13. Panel Illumination, Panel Dimmer, Panel Lights
This control, usually continuously variable, controls all panel lamps. In some cases this includes the digital data readouts and the bearing scales.

14. Input Speed Selector, Manual/Log
This switch permits selection of either manual or ship's log input speed for use with ARPA.

15. Ship's Speed, Manual Speed, Manual Log, Input
This control is usually a thumbwheel switch or an indicator type switch. The switch reads in knots and tenths of a knot and is used for manual input of speed when your ship's log input is not available or is inoperative.

16. Function Switch, North/Head Up, Mode Selector
This control permits selection of either north-up or head-up display orientation. The north-up position displays all targets in their true chart position. Head up displays your ship on a heading of 0° with all targets displayed on the PPI in the same relative plan positions as they are seen from your ship's bridge.

17. Future Position, Vector Time
This control sets the length of target vectors and maintains length proportional to your ship's chosen speed and time.

18. Plot Selector, TM/RM Select
This control selects CRT display to be either true or relative motion. Target-tracking functions are operative in either mode.

19. CPA Distance, CPA Alarm
By actuating this control, the projected CPA distance of all targets is monitored continously. When the CPA of any target is calculated to be within the limit set on this switch (and also within the Time-to-CPA set on the related control), the automatic and visual alarms are actuated.

20. TCPA (Time-to-CPA) Alarm Set
Use this control, if the target's CPA distance and TCPA are less than the set values, and the audio and visual alarm is actuated. When traffic is dense, smaller values will normally be selected. Reducing the control setting quickly shows which threat is the most urgent if more than one target is present in an alarm situation.

21. CPA Alarm Light, Alarms Group, Target Danger
A warning light is automatically actuated when a target is predicted to violate the CPA and TCPA limits set on these controls.

22. Fault Alarm, System Failure, Fault Warning
An indicator will light and an audio signal will sound when the self-check circuitry indicates that the ARPA is for some reason not processing radar-received echoes.

23. Trial Maneuver
This control selects a trial mode to allow results of proposed maneuvers to be assessed. The trial is displayed on the CRT during that period. At the same time, however, the ARPA is solving the real-time situation, and will display it the instant the trial maneuver is completed.

24. Trial Speed

This control allows you to set a proposed trial speed in one-knot increments prior to executing a trial maneuver.

25. Trial Course

This control allows you to set a trial, true course maneuver in degrees. (See No. 23, Trial Maneuver, above.)

26. Time to Maneuver, Trial Time

This control allows you to fully analyze the time it takes to complete a maneuver before executing it. The information it displays takes into consideration the delay involved in starting the maneuver action and includes the time to complete the action based on your ship's maneuvering characteristics.

27. Minimum Tracking Range

This control, usually a thumbwheel switch, eliminates all targets within the range setting. Targets which had been acquired are therefore erased from the display. This control allows for the quick elimination of unwanted targets, i.e., clutter, from the display. Minimum tracking range is normally set for zero range. When it is extreme at close range, clutter may result in dotting, or an extended target indication on the display when the Video Gain control is turned to the *land* detent position. Setting *minimum tracking range* to a value equal to the range of the dotting will eliminate this problem. Adjustment of radar STC and gain will also eliminate this heavy clutter problem and is preferable, for any setting of minimum tracking range eliminates all targets within this range.

TABLE 1. DISTANCE IN NAUTICAL MILES BY TIME AND SPEED

Time in Minutes

Speed in Knots	1	2	3	6	9	12	15	18	21
2	.03	.07	.1	.2	.3	.4	.5	.6	.7
4	.07	.13	.2	.4	.6	.8	1.0	1.2	1.4
6	.1	.2	.3	.6	.9	1.2	1.5	1.8	2.1
8	.13	.27	.4	.8	1.2	1.6	2.0	2.4	2.8
10	.17	.33	.5	1.0	1.5	2.0	2.5	3.0	3.5
12	.2	.4	.6	1.2	1.8	2.4	3.0	3.6	4.2
14	.23	.47	.7	1.4	2.1	2.8	3.5	4.2	4.9
16	.27	.53	.8	1.6	2.4	3.2	4.0	4.8	5.6
18	.3	.6	.9	1.8	2.7	3.6	4.5	5.4	6.3
20	.33	.66	1.0	2.0	3.0	4.0	5.0	6.0	7.0
25	.42	.83	1.25	2.5	3.8	5.0	6.3	7.5	8.8
30	.5	1.0	1.5	3.0	4.5	6.0	7.5	9.0	10.5

TABLE 2. LOGARITHMIC TIME-SPEED-DISTANCE SCALES

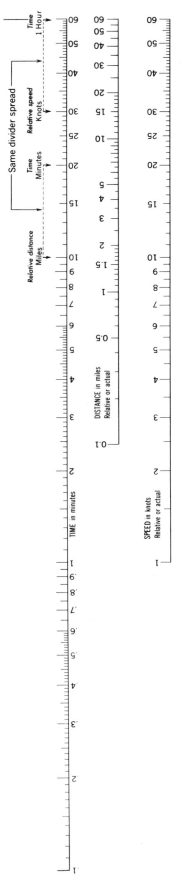

LOGARITHMIC TIME, SPEED, AND DISTANCE SCALE

TO FIND SPEED, place one point of dividers on elapsed time and second point on distance in miles. Without changing spread of dividers or right-left relationship of points, place first point on 60; second point will then indicate speed in knots.

TO FIND DISTANCE OR TIME, place one point of dividers on 60 and second point on speed in knots. Without changing spread of dividers or right-left relationship of points, place first point on time; second point will then indicate distance in miles. Or, place second point on distance in miles; first point will then indicate time.

Actual distance and speed units can be used in the same way as relative units.

USE OF 3-SCALE NOMOGRAM

Given any two corresponding quantities, solve for third by laying rule through points on proper scales and read intersection on third scale.